HOLT McDOUGAL

Geometry

COMMON CORE **State Standards Curriculum Companion**

Student Edition

Edward B. Burger

David J. Chard

Paul A. Kennedy

Steven J. Leinwand

Freddie L. Renfro

Tom W. Roby

Dale G. Seymour

Bert K. Waits

HOLT McDOUGAL

HOUGHTON MIFFLIN HARCOURT

Cover photo: © Micha Pawlitzki/Corbis

Geometry Common Core State Standards Curriculum Companion

Student Edition

Contents

Congruence and Transformations

Objectives
Draw, identify, and describe transformations in the coordinate plane.

Use properties of rigid motions to determine whether figures are congruent and to prove figures congruent.

Vocabulary
dilation
isometry
rigid transformation

Why learn this?
Transformations can be used to create frieze patterns in art and architecture, such as in this cast iron gate.

A transformation is a change in the position, shape, or size of a figure. Some types of transformations are translations (slides), reflections (flips), rotations (turns), and *dilations*.

A **dilation** with scale factor $k > 0$ and center $(0, 0)$ maps (x, y) to (kx, ky).

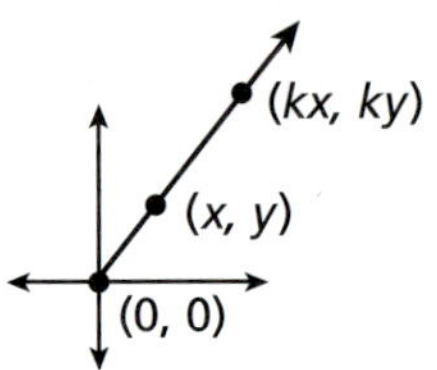

EXAMPLE 1

Drawing and Identifying Transformations

Apply the transformation M to the polygon with the given vertices. Identify and describe the transformation.

A $M : (x, y) \rightarrow (x + 2, y - 5)$
$P(1, 2),\ Q(4, 4),\ R(4, 2)$

This is a translation 2 units right and 5 units down.

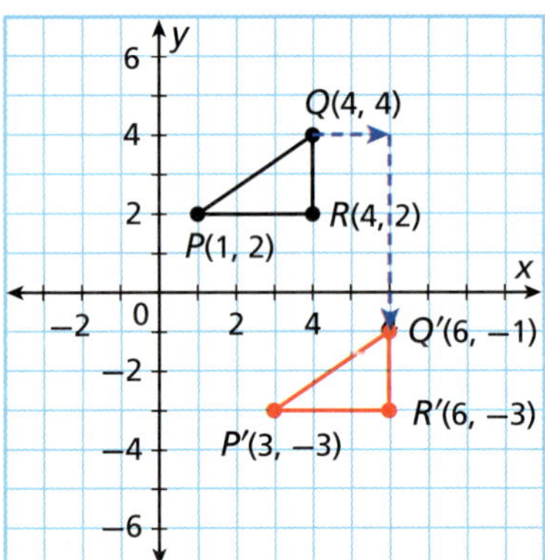

Remember!

In a transformation, the original figure is the preimage. The resulting figure is the image.

B $M : (x, y) \rightarrow (-x, y)$
$A(1, 1),\ B(3, 2),\ C(3, 5)$

This is a reflection across the y-axis.

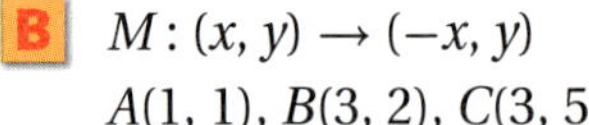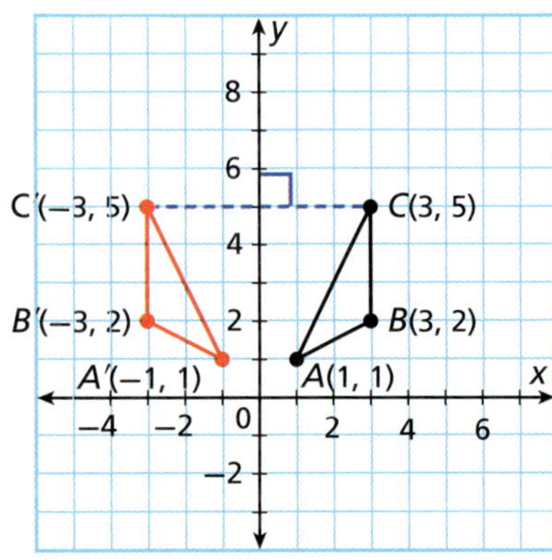

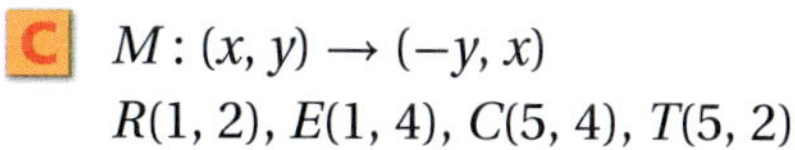

C $M : (x, y) \rightarrow (-y, x)$
$R(1, 2), E(1, 4), C(5, 4), T(5, 2)$

This is a 90° rotation counterclockwise with center of rotation (0, 0).

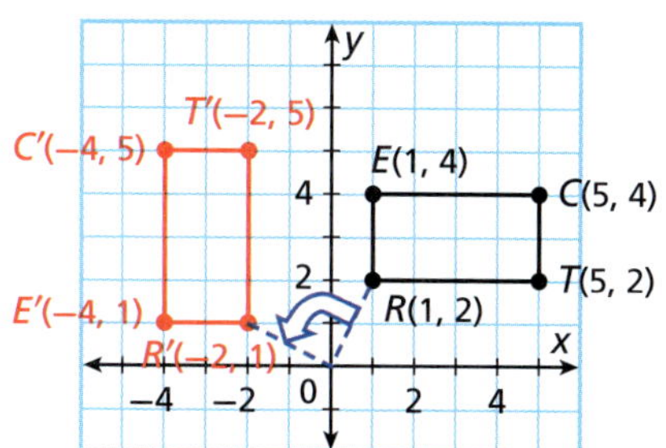

D $M : (x, y) \rightarrow (2x, 2y)$
$K(-1, 2), L(2, 2), N(1, 3)$

This is a dilation with scale factor 2 and center (0, 0).

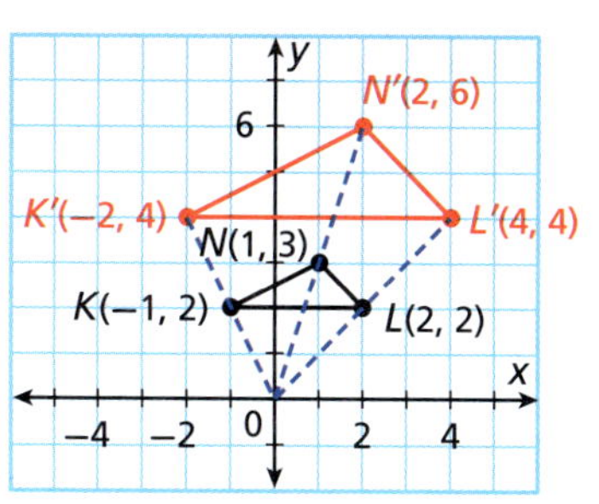

1. Apply the transformation $M : (x, y) \rightarrow (3x, 3y)$ to the polygon with vertices $D(1, 3)$, $E(1, -2)$, and $F(3, 0)$. Name the coordinates of the image points. Identify and describe the transformation.

Representing Transformations in the Coordinate Plane

TRANSFORMATION	COORDINATE MAPPING AND DESCRIPTION
Translation	$(x, y) \rightarrow (x + a, y + b)$ Translation a units horizontally and b units vertically
Reflection	$(x, y) \rightarrow (-x, y)$ Reflection across y-axis $(x, y) \rightarrow (x, -y)$ Reflection across x-axis
Rotation	$(x, y) \rightarrow (y, -x)$ Rotation about (0, 0), 90° clockwise $(x, y) \rightarrow (-y, x)$ Rotation about (0, 0), 90° counterclockwise $(x, y) \rightarrow (-x, -y)$ Rotation about (0, 0), 180°
Dilation	$(x, y) \rightarrow (kx, ky), k > 0$ Dilation with scale factor k and center (0, 0)

An **isometry** is a transformation that preserves length, angle measure, and area. Because of these properties, an isometry produces an image that is congruent to the preimage. A **rigid transformation** is another name for an isometry.

Transformations and Congruence

Translations, reflections, and rotations produce images that are congruent to their preimages.

Dilations with scale factor $k \neq 1$ produce images that are not congruent to their preimages.

You can determine whether some figures are congruent by determining what type of transformation(s) can be applied to one figure to produce the other figure.

EXAMPLE 2 Determining Whether Figures are Congruent

Determine whether the polygons with the given vertices are congruent.

A $A(1, 1)$, $B(4, 1)$, $C(4, 3)$
$P(-4, 2)$, $Q(-1, 2)$, $R(-1, 4)$

The triangles are congruent because $\triangle ABC$ can be mapped to $\triangle PQR$ by a translation:

$(x, y) \rightarrow (x - 5, y + 1)$.

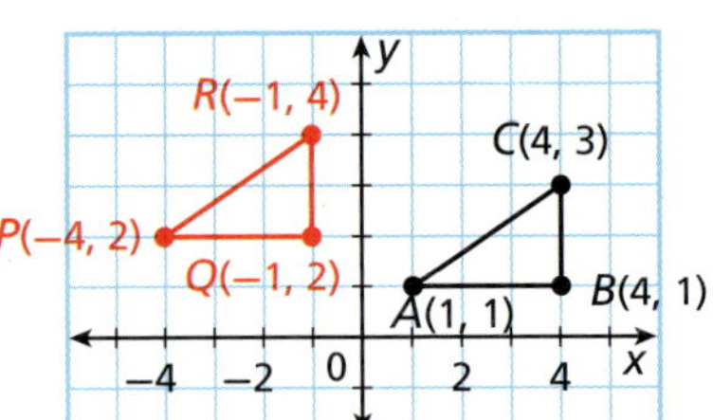

B $A(2, 2)$, $B(-4, 4)$, $C(2, 4)$
$P(3, 3)$, $Q(-6, 6)$, $R(3, 6)$

The triangles are not congruent because $\triangle ABC$ can be mapped to $\triangle PQR$ by a dilation with scale factor $k \neq 1$:

$(x, y) \rightarrow (1.5x, 1.5y)$.

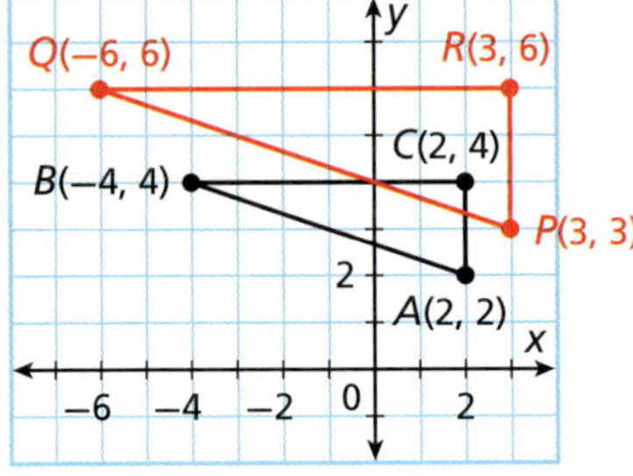

2. Determine whether the polygons with the given vertices are congruent. Support your answer by describing a transformation: $A(2, -1)$, $B(3, 0)$, $C(2, 3)$ and $P(1, 2)$, $Q(0, 3)$, $R(-3, 2)$.

You can prove two figures are congruent by showing there are one or more translations, reflections, or rotations that map one figure to the other.

EXAMPLE 3 Applying Transformations

Prove that the polygons with the given vertices are congruent.

$A(3, 1)$, $B(2, -1)$, $C(7, -1)$
$P(-3, -2)$, $Q(-5, -1)$, $R(-5, -6)$

Graph the triangles. There is no apparent single transformation that maps $\triangle ABC$ to $\triangle PQR$. Look for a combination of congruence transformations that map $\triangle ABC$ to $\triangle PQR$.

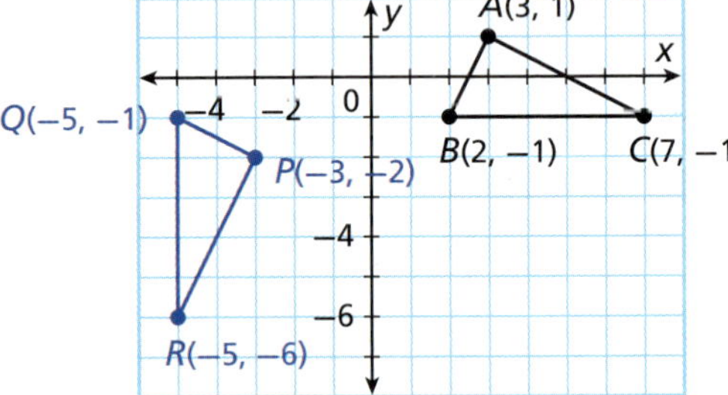

The triangles are congruent because $\triangle ABC$ can be mapped to $\triangle A'B'C'$ by a translation:

$(x, y) \rightarrow (x - 1, y - 4)$; and $\triangle A'B'C'$ can then be mapped to $\triangle PQR$ by a rotation:

$(x, y) \rightarrow (y, -x)$.

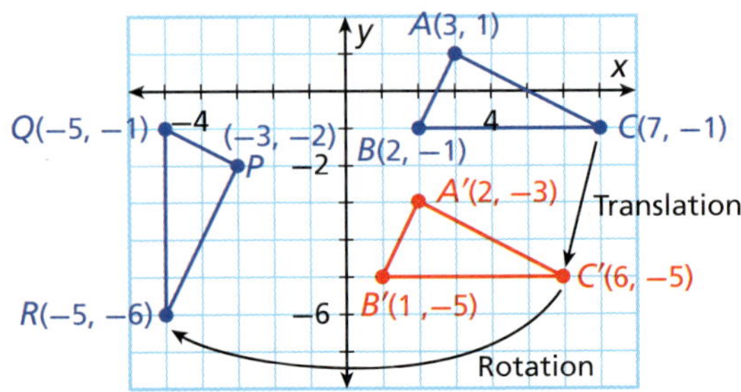

3. Prove that the polygons with the given vertices are congruent:
$A(-4, -2)$, $B(-2, 1)$, $C(-2, -2)$ and $P(1, 0)$, $Q(3, -3)$, $R(3, 0)$.

E X A M P L E 4 *Architecture Application*

What transformation is used to create the frieze pattern in this cast iron gate? Are sections of the gate congruent? Explain your answer.

Repeated horizontal translations create the frieze pattern. A translation of any section either to the left or to the right by a distance equal to the width of the section produces an image that is congruent to the preimage.

Helpful Hint

Translations, reflections, and rotations can be called congruence transformations.

4. Sketch a frieze pattern that can be produced by using reflections.

THINK AND DISCUSS

1. Think of the transformation mapping $(x, y) \rightarrow (x + 5, y - 2)$ as a function with input (x, y). What is the output of the function? If the transformation is applied to a polygon, describe the size, shape, and position of the image compared to the preimage.

2. What type of transformation preserves angle but does not preserve distance?

3. Describe a dilation with center $(0, 0)$ that would produce an image such that every image point is closer to $(0, 0)$ than its corresponding preimage point.

4. GET ORGANIZED
Copy and complete the graphic organizer, including coordinate transformation rules.

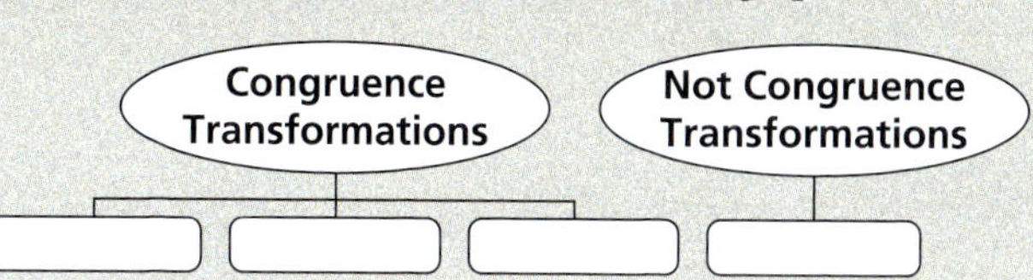

4-1A Exercises

GUIDED PRACTICE

Vocabulary Apply the vocabulary from this lesson to answer each question.

1. Dilations with scale factor $k \neq 1$ produce images that ____?___ (*are, are not*) congruent to their preimages.

2. An ____?___ (*isometry, image*) is a transformation that preserves length, angle, and area; it is also called a ____?___ (*translation, rigid transformation*).

SEE EXAMPLE 1
p. CC2

Apply the transformation M to the polygon with the given vertices. Name the coordinates of the image points. Identify and describe the transformation.

3. $M: (x, y) \rightarrow (x, -y)$
$A(2, 1), B(5, 4), C(5, 1)$

4. $M: (x, y) \rightarrow (3x, 3y)$
$P(-2, 1), Q(-1, 2), R(0, 1)$

5. $M: (x, y) \rightarrow (y, -x)$
$L(3, 1), M(3, 4), N(5, 4), O(5, 1)$

6. $M: (x, y) \rightarrow (x - 3, y + 2)$
$D(4, -1), E(7, 3), F(7, -1)$

SEE EXAMPLE 2
p. CC4

Determine whether the polygons with the given vertices are congruent. Support your answer by describing a transformation.

7. $A(-4, 4), B(-4, 6), C(2, 6), D(2, 4)$ and $W(-2, 2), X(-2, 3), Y(1, 3), Z(1, 2)$

8. $A(-2, -2), B(-4, -1), C(-1, -1)$ and $T(2, 2), U(4, 1), V(1, 1)$

SEE EXAMPLE 3
p. CC4

Prove that the polygons with the given vertices are congruent.

9. $J(-5, 2), K(-2, 5), L(-2, 2)$ and $M(5, 0), N(2, 3), O(2, 0)$

10. $D(-1, -5), E(-4, -4), F(-1, -2)$ and $X(3, 4), Y(6, 3), Z(3, 1)$

SEE EXAMPLE 4
p. CC5

11. Victorian Crafts What transformation is used to create the frieze pattern in the wallpaper shown? Are there any congruent sections of the wallpaper? Explain your answer.

12. Sketch a frieze pattern that can be produced by using reflections and/or translations.

PRACTICE AND PROBLEM SOLVING

Independent Practice	
For Exercises	See Example
13–18	1
19–21	2
22–24	3
25	4

Apply the transformation M to the polygon with the given vertices. Name the coordinates of the image points. Identify and describe the transformation.

13. $M: (x, y) \rightarrow (x + 5, y - 4)$
$G(4, -1), H(7, 3), I(7, -1)$

14. $M: (x, y) \rightarrow (-x, y)$
$P(3, 2), Q(6, 2), R(3, 5)$

15. $M: (x, y) \rightarrow (1.5x, 1.5y)$
$L(-1, 4), M(-4, 4), N(-4, 3)$

16. $M: (x, y) \rightarrow (-y, x)$
$A(-7, 6), B(-7, 4), C(-4, 6), D(-4, 4)$

17. $M: (x, y) \rightarrow (x - 1, y + 1)$
$N(1, -2), O(0, 4), P(2, 4)$

18. $M: (x, y) \rightarrow (-x, -y)$
$W(5, 2), X(2, 2), Y(5, 5)$

Determine whether the polygons with the given vertices are congruent. Support your answer by describing a transformation.

19. $J(-4, 4), K(-4, 6), L(2, 6), M(2, 4)$ and $A(4, 4), B(6, 4), C(6, -2), D(4, -2)$

20. $P(-2, -2), Q(-4, -1), R(-1, -1)$ and $X(2, 2), Y(4, 1), Z(1, 1)$

21. $E(-1, -1), F(2, 2), G(-3, 3)$ and $U(-1, 2), V(2, 5), W(-3, 6)$

Prove that the polygons with the given vertices are congruent.

22. $D(-5, -1), E(-2, 1), F(2, -1)$ and $X(-1, 1), Y(2, -1), Z(6, 1)$

23. $A(2, -1), B(4, -2), C(6, 0)$ and $D(-3, -2), E(-4, -4), F(-2, -6)$

24. $P(-7, 3), Q(-8, 7), R(-4, 7)$ and $G(4, -3), H(5, -7), I(1, -7)$

25. Quilting Jennifer is designing a quilt. She made this diagram to follow when making her quilt.

   a. What transformation or combination of transformations is used to create the pattern in this quilt design?

   b. Are sections of the quilt congruent? Explain your answer.

   c. What if ... ? How might the design look different if she had used 180° rotations instead?

Apply the transformation M to the polygon with the given vertices. Name the coordinates of the image points. Identify and describe the transformation.

26. $M: (x, y) \to (x - 3, y + 2)$

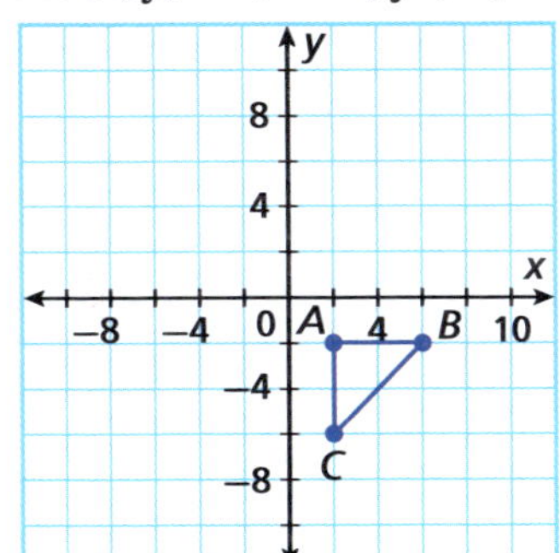

27. $M: (x, y) \to (y, -x)$

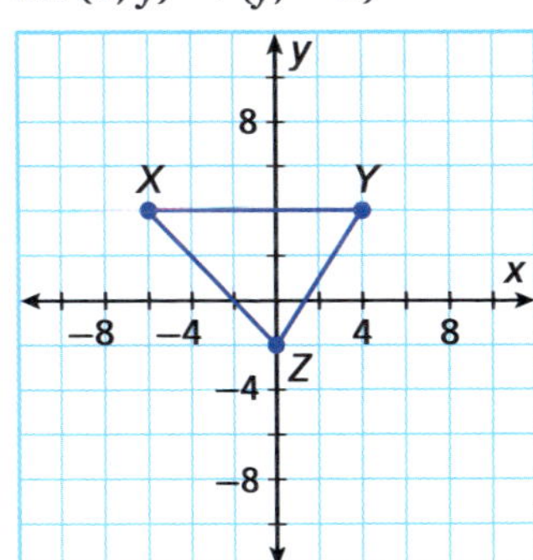

28. Logo Design Eli made this logo design for a company letterhead. What transformation(s) did he use to make the design? Are there any congruent shapes in the design?

Apply the transformations M to the polygon with the given vertices. Name the coordinates of the image points. Identify and describe the transformations.

29. $M: (x, y) \to (x, -y) \to (x + 3, y)$

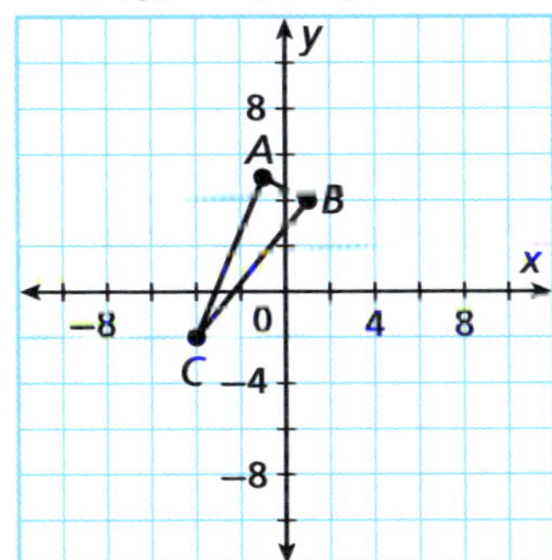

30. $M: (x, y) \to (3x, 3y) \to (-y, x)$

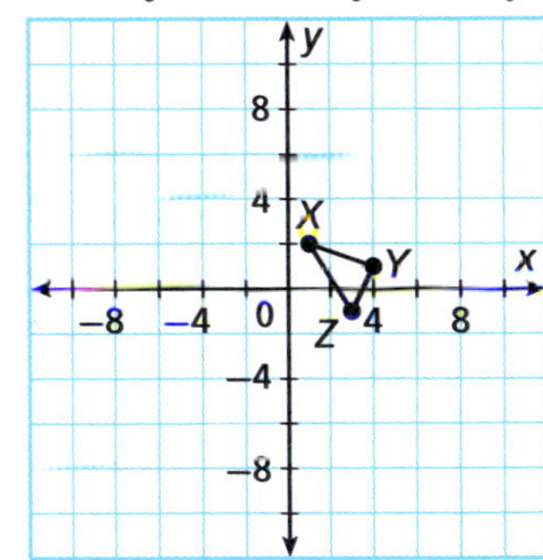

31. **Tessellations** Frank developed a tessellating shape to use in a repeating design. Describe the series of transformations he used to create this square design of his tessellated shape.

32. **Signal Flags** Seth is going to recreate this signal flag out of fabric. He has light blue and dark blue fabric. What transformations will he perform on the light blue triangles to position them correctly, if he starts in the upper left corner?

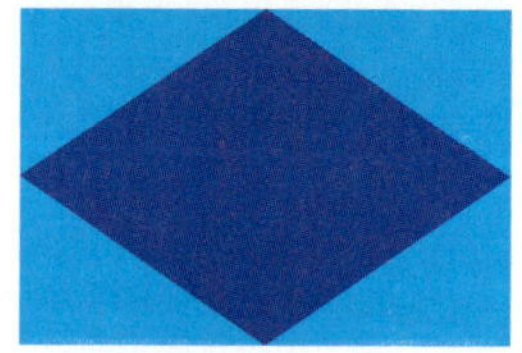

33. **///ERROR ANALYSIS///** Erin and Dave are looking at the triangles on the coordinate plane shown. They are each trying to prove that the triangles are congruent. Who has the correct answer? Explain why.

Erin's Answer
The triangles are congruent because △ABC can be mapped to △DEF by a rotation: $(x, y) \rightarrow (-y, x)$. Then △DEF can be mapped to △XYZ by a translation: $(x, y) \rightarrow (x + 2, y + 3)$.

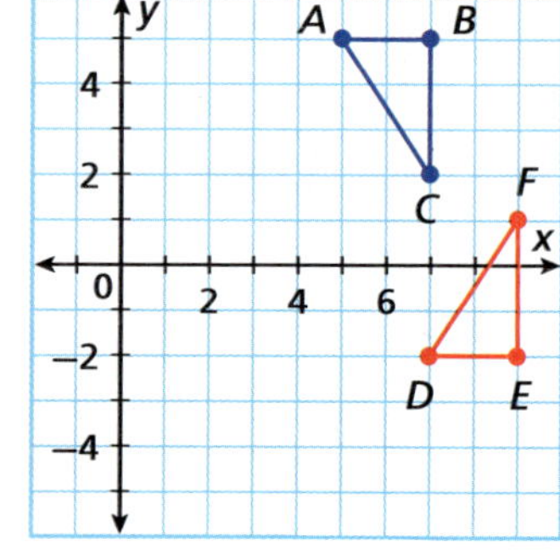

Dave's Answer
The triangles are congruent because △ABC can be mapped to △DEF by a reflection: $(x, y) \rightarrow (x, -y)$. Then △DEF can be mapped to △XYZ by a translation: $(x, y) \rightarrow (x + 2, y + 3)$.

34. **Write About It** Describe the differences in reflecting a polygon and rotating a polygon in terms of the coordinate mapping directions.

35. **Critical Thinking** How does a dilation of a figure with scale factor 0.5 compare to a dilation of the figure with scale factor 2? Explain.

36. Alex is trying two transformations that will map the preimage to the image.
$D(-5, -2)$, $E(-2, -2)$, $F(-4, -5)$ and $X(10, -4)$, $Y(4, -4)$, $Z(8, -10)$
Which two transformations should he choose?
   Ⓐ translation and reflection
   Ⓑ dilation and reflection
   Ⓒ reflection and rotation
   Ⓓ rotation and dilation

37. Bill applied the transformation *M* to the polygon. What are the coordinates of the image points for the polygon?

M: $(x, y) \rightarrow (x, -y)$

  Ⓐ $A'(1, 1)$, $B'(6, 4)$, $C'(8, -2)$

  Ⓑ $A'(-1, 1)$, $B'(-6, 4)$, $C'(-8, -2)$

  Ⓒ $A'(-1, -1)$, $B'(-6, -4)$, $C'(-8, 2)$

  Ⓓ $A'(1, -1)$, $B'(6, -4)$, $C'(8, 2)$

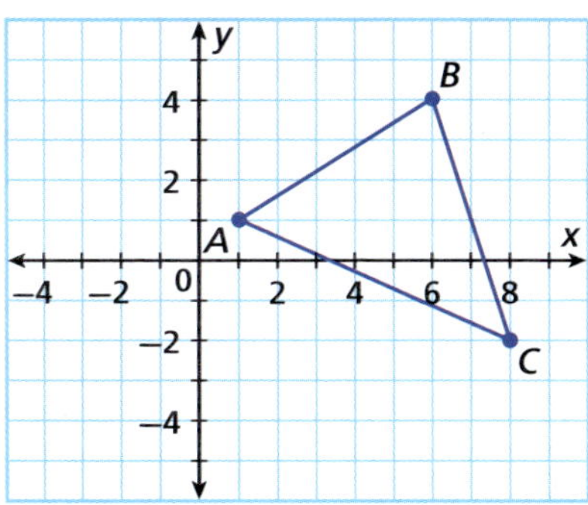

CHALLENGE AND EXTEND

38. Architecture Steve was visiting the ruins at Mitla, an archeological site in Mexico. He saw this frieze design.

  a. Does the frieze have congruent shapes? What transformation or combination of tranformations are used to create the pattern in this frieze design?

  b. **What if … ?** How might the design have looked if the designers had rotated the S-shapes 90 degrees clockwise and then translated an entire row to make the next row? Sketch your answer.

SPIRAL REVIEW

Find the measure of each of the following. *(Lesson 1-4)*

39. supplement of $\angle A$

40. complement of $\angle A$

41. supplement of $\angle B$

42. complement of $\angle B$

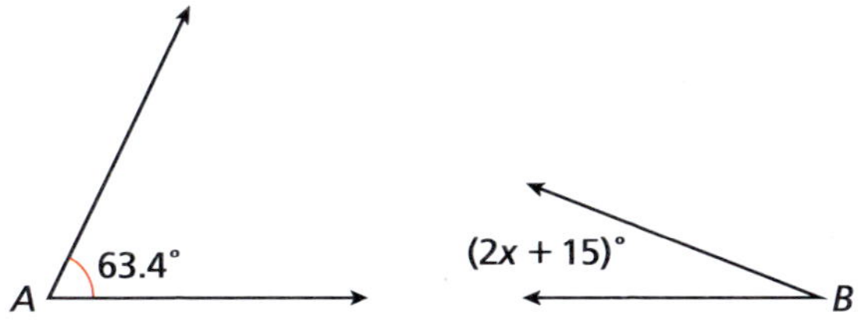

Find the coordinates of the midpoint of each segment. *(Lesson 1-6)*

43. $\overline{CD}$ with endpoints $C(3, -2)$ and $D(5, 3)$

44. $\overline{JK}$ with endpoints $J(-4, 0)$ and $K(0, 6)$

Give an example of each angle pair. *(Lesson 3-1)*

45. alternate interior angles

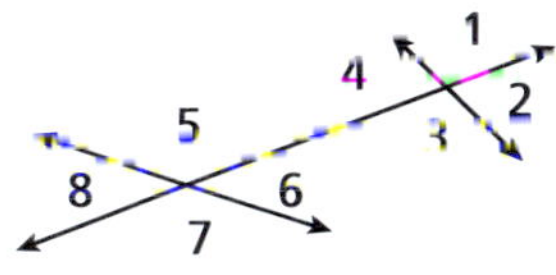

46. alternate exterior angles

47. corresponding angles

48. same-side interior angles

Lines and Slopes

Objective
Prove the slope criteria for parallel and perpendicular lines.

Slopes can be used to determine if two lines in a coordinate plane are parallel or perpendicular. In this lesson, you will prove the Parallel Lines Theorem and the Perpendicular Lines Theorem. Suppose that L_1 and L_2 are two lines in the coordinate plane with slopes m_1 and m_2. The proof of the Parallel Lines Theorem can be broken into three parts:

1. If $L_1 \parallel L_2$ and L_1 and L_2 are not vertical, then $m_1 = m_2$.
2. If $m_1 = m_2$, then $L_1 \parallel L_2$.
3. If L_1 and L_2 are vertical, then $L_1 \parallel L_2$.

EXAMPLE **1** **Proving the Parallel Lines Theorem**

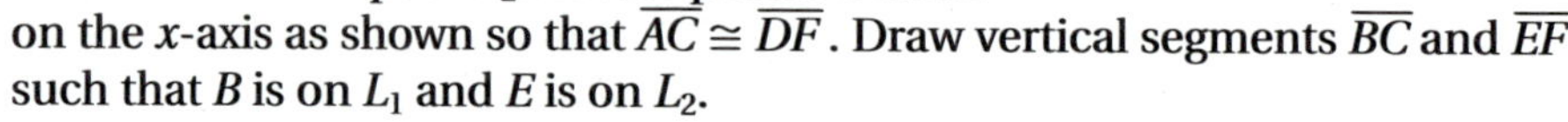

Given: $L_1 \parallel L_2$, L_1 and L_2 are not vertical
Prove: $m_1 = m_2$
Proof:

Assume that L_1 and L_2 are not horizontal. Locate point A at the x-intercept of L_1 and point D at the x-intercept of L_2. Locate points C and F on the x-axis as shown so that $\overline{AC} \cong \overline{DF}$. Draw vertical segments $\overline{BC}$ and $\overline{EF}$ such that B is on L_1 and E is on L_2.

The x-axis is a transversal to L_1 and L_2, and it is given that $L_1 \parallel L_2$, so $\angle BAC \cong \angle EDF$ by the Corresponding Angles Postulate. By construction, $\overline{AC} \cong \overline{DF}$, and $\angle ACB$ and $\angle DFE$ are right angles, so $\angle ACB \cong \angle DFE$. Therefore, $\triangle ABC \cong \triangle DEF$ by ASA congruence. Because CPCTC, $\overline{BC} \cong \overline{EF}$.

By the definition of congruent segments, $AC = DF$ and $BC = EF$. By the Substitution Property of Equality and the definition of slope,
$$m_1 = \frac{BC}{AC} = \frac{EF}{DF} = m_2.$$

1. Complete the two-column proof, using the figure in Example 1.
Given: $m_1 = m_2$
Prove: $L_1 \parallel L_2$
Proof:

Statements	Reasons
1. $m_1 = m_2$	1. ___?___
2. $\dfrac{BC}{AC} = \dfrac{EF}{DF}$	2. ___?___
3. $AC = DF$	3. By construction
4. $\dfrac{BC}{AC} = \dfrac{EF}{AC}$	4. ___?___
5. $BC = EF$	5. ___?___
6. $\angle ACB \cong \angle DFE$	6. By construction, all right angles are $\cong$
7. $\triangle ABC \cong \triangle DEF$	7. ___?___
8. $\angle BAC \cong \angle EDF$	8. ___?___
9. $L_1 \parallel L_2$	9. ___?___

The proof of the Perpendicular Lines Theorem can be broken into three parts:

1. If $L_1 \perp L_2$ and L_1 and L_2 are not vertical, then $m_1 m_2 = -1$.
2. If $m_1 m_2 = -1$, then $L_1 \perp L_2$.
3. If L_1 is horizontal and L_2 is vertical, then $L_1 \perp L_2$.

The third statement will be used in the proof of the second statement. Proof of the third statement is left as an exercise.

EXAMPLE 2 Proving the Perpendicular Lines

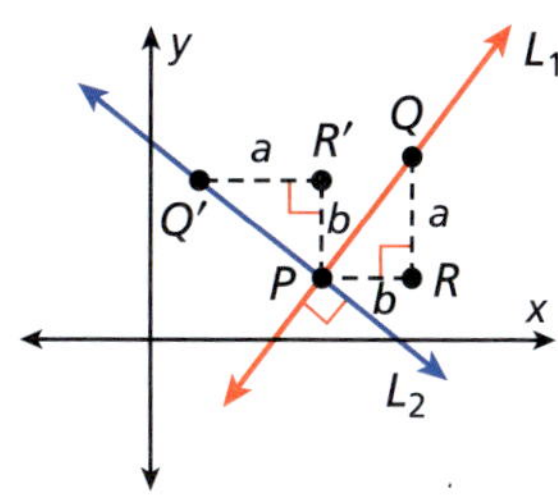

Given: $L_1 \perp L_2$, L_1 and L_2 are not vertical
Prove: $m_1 m_2 = -1$
Proof:

Suppose that $m_1 = \frac{a}{b}$ and that L_1 and L_2 intersect at point P. Draw a right triangle $\triangle PQR$ with side $\overline{PQ}$ on L_1, where $\overline{PR}$ is a horizontal side of length b representing the run, and $\overline{QR}$ is a vertical side of length a representing the rise.

Rotate $\triangle PQR$ by 90° counterclockwise around point P to form the image $\triangle PQ'R'$. Because $L_1 \perp L_2$, the image Q' will lie on point L_2. $\overline{PR'}$ is a 90° rotation of $\overline{PR}$, so it is vertical with length b, and $\overline{QR'}$ is a 90° rotation of $\overline{QR}$ so it is horizontal, with length a.

The slope of L_2 is $m_2 = \frac{-b}{a}$, so $m_1 m_2 = \frac{a}{b}\left(\frac{-b}{a}\right) = -1$.

2. Complete the paragraph proof below.
Given: $m1 \cdot m2 = -1$
Prove: $L1 \perp L2$
Proof:

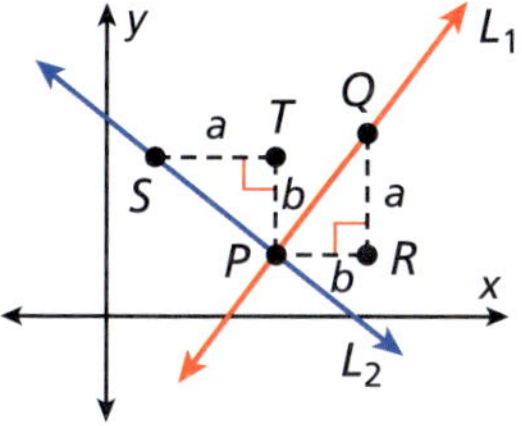

Let $m_1 = \frac{a}{b}$. Then $m_2 = -\frac{b}{a}$. Draw PQR with sides of length a and b and a right angle at R to represent the rise and run of L_1, and $\triangle PST$ with sides of length b and a to represent the rise and run of L_2.

$\triangle PQR \cong \triangle PST$ by **a.__?__**, so $\angle QPR \cong \angle SPT$ because **b.__?__**.

$m\angle QPR = m\angle SPT$ by **c.__?__**.

By construction, $\overline{PT} \perp \overline{PR}$, so $m\angle RPT = 90°$ by the definition of perpendicular lines.

$m\angle QPT + m\angle QPR = 90°$ by **e.__?__**.

Then $m\angle QPT + m\angle SPT = 90°$ by **f.__?__**, so $m\angle SPQ = 90°$ by **g.__?__**.

$L_1 \perp L_2$ by **h.__?__**.

Determine whether the lines shown are parallel, perpendicular, or neither.

1.

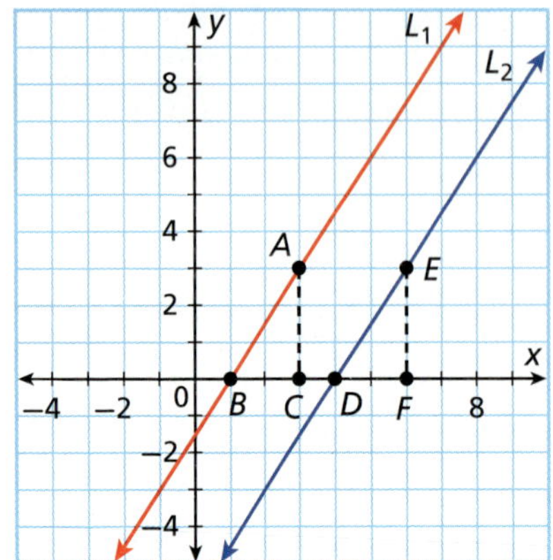

2.

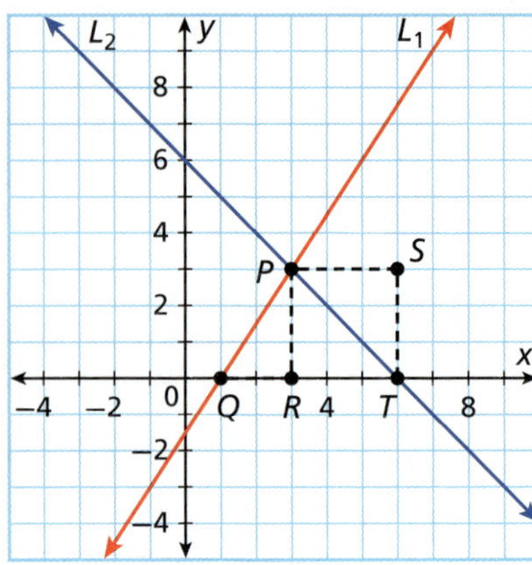

3.

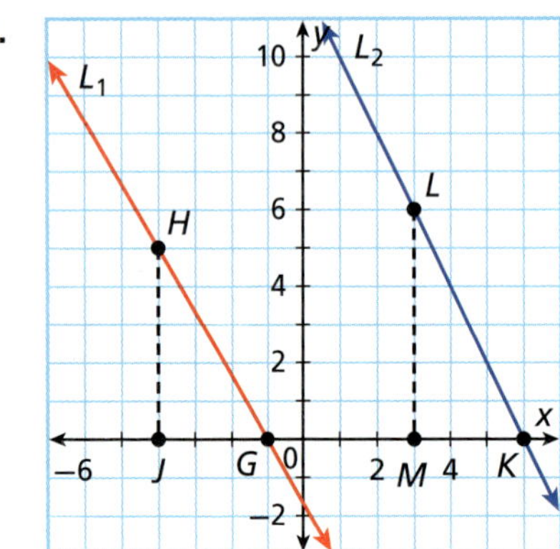

4.

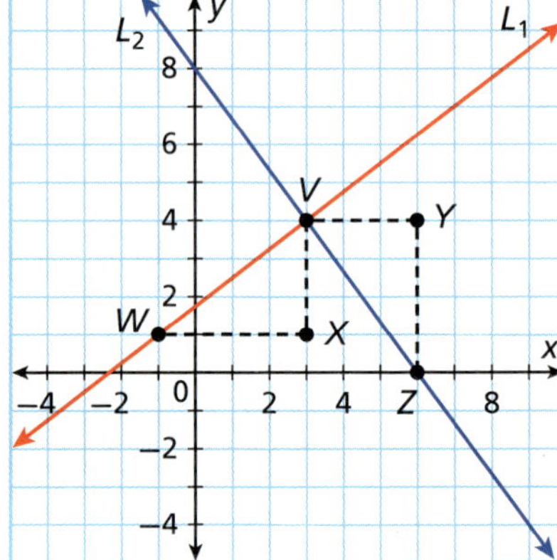

5. The coordinate plane shows two lines. Determine whether or not the lines are perpendicular. Explain your answer.

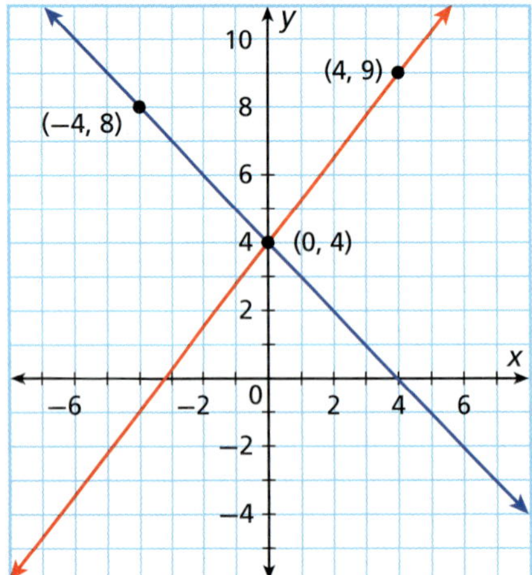

6. The coordinate plane shows two lines. Determine whether or not the lines are parallel. Explain your answer.

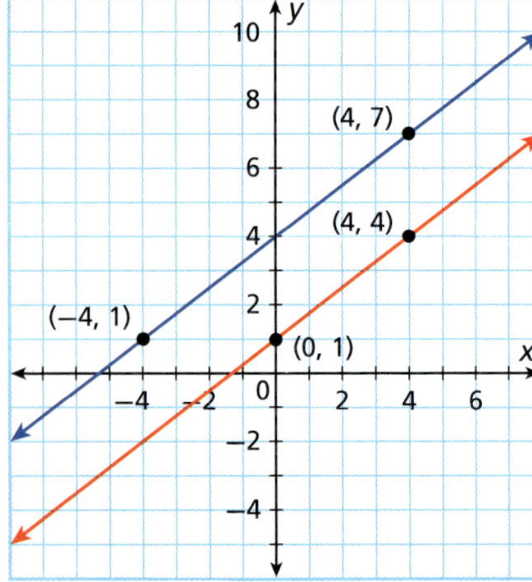

7. Find the equation of the line parallel to the line shown that passes through the point $(4, 8)$.

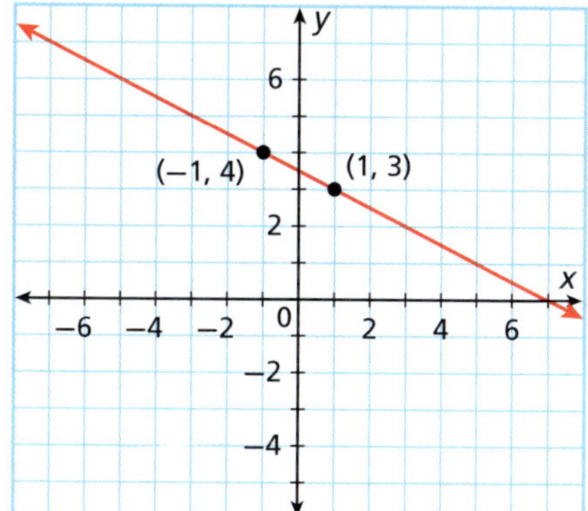

8. Find the equation of the line perpendicular to the line shown that passes through the point $(-3, 1)$.

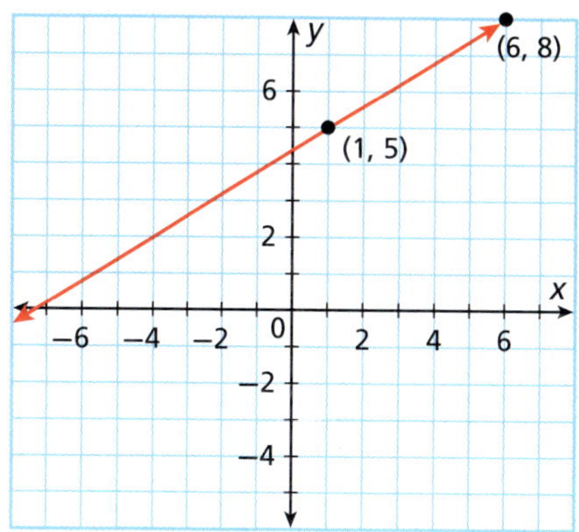

Challenge Prove the remaining parts of the Parallel Lines Theorem and Perpendicular Lines Theorem below. You may use the reasons below in your proofs.

- **Definition of coordinate plane:** The coordinate plane is divided into four regions by two perpendicular lines, called the x-axis and the y-axis.
- **Definition of horizontal line:** A horizontal line is parallel to the x-axis.
- **Definition of vertical line:** A vertical line is parallel to the y-axis.

9. **Given:** L_1 and L_2 with $m_1 = m_2 = 0$
Prove: $L_1 \parallel L_2$

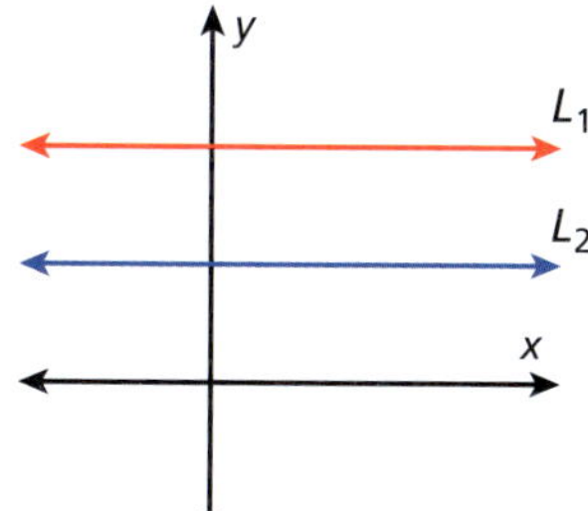

10. **Given:** L_1 and L_2 are vertical.
Prove: $L_1 \parallel L_2$

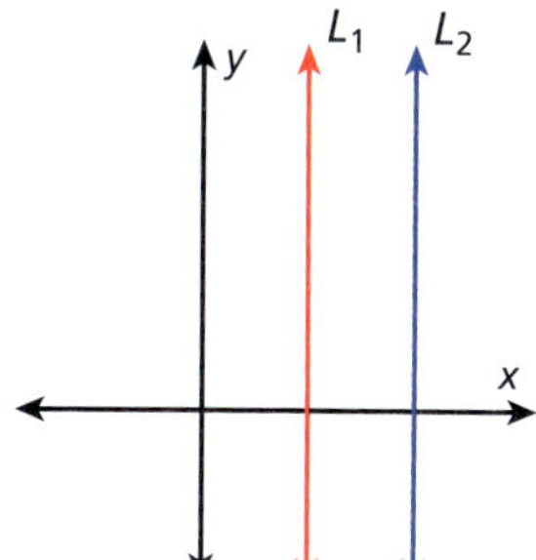

11. **Given:** L_1 is horizontal and L_2 is vertical
Prove: $L_1 \perp L_2$

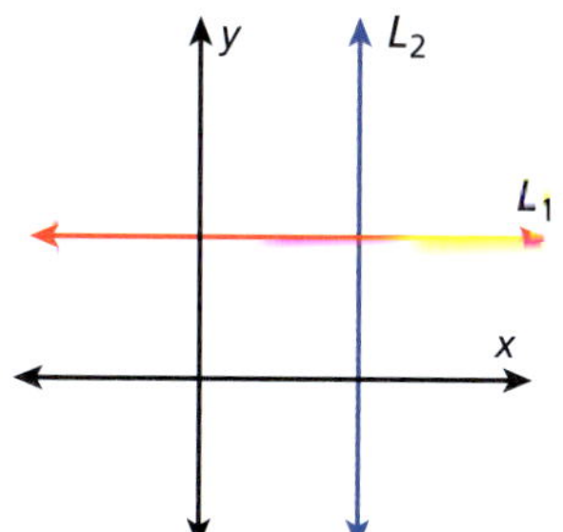

Similarity and Transformations

Objectives
Draw and describe similarity transformations in the coordinate plane.

Use properties of similarity transformations to determine whether polygons are similar and to prove circles are similar.

Vocabulary
similarity transformation

Who uses this?

A sign maker can use a similarity transformation to create a banner showing state flags. (See Example 4.)

A transformation that maps (x, y) to (kx, ky), where $k > 0$, is a dilation with center $(0, 0)$ and scale factor k. If $0 < k < 1$, the dilation is a *reduction*. If $k > 1$, the dilation is an *enlargement*.

Jürgen Priewe/Alamy

EXAMPLE **1**

Drawing and Describing Dilations

Apply the dilation D to the polygon with the given vertices. Describe the dilation.

A $D : (x, y) \rightarrow (2x, 2y)$

$A(2, 1), B(2, 3), C(5, 1)$

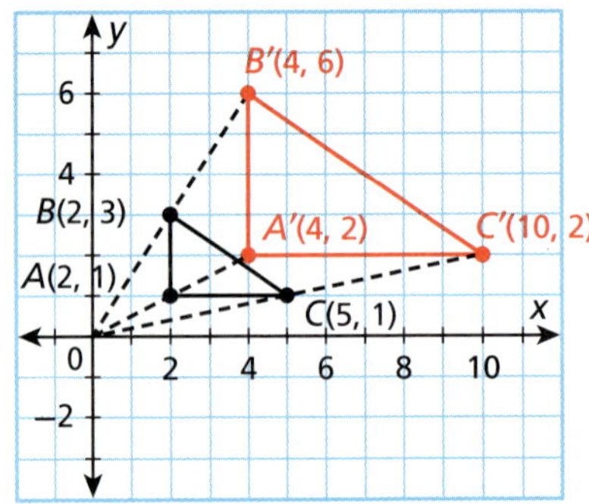

This is a dilation with center $(0, 0)$ and scale factor 2.

B $D : (x, y) \rightarrow \left(\frac{2}{3}x, \frac{2}{3}y\right)$

$P(-6, 3), Q(-3, 9), R(3, 6)$

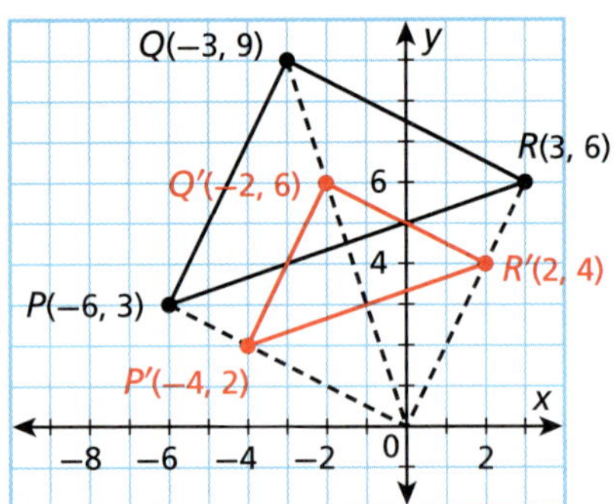

This is a dilation with center $(0, 0)$ and scale factor $\frac{2}{3}$.

1. Apply the dilation $D : (x, y) \rightarrow \left(\frac{1}{4}x, \frac{1}{4}y\right)$ to the polygon with vertices $D(-8, 0)$, $E(-8, -4)$, and $F(-4, -8)$. Name the coordinates of the image points. Describe the dilation.

Remember!

Translations, reflections, and rotations are congruence transformations.

In a dilation, the image and the preimage are similar because they have the same shape. When the figures in a dilation are polygons, the image and preimage are similar polygons, so corresponding side lengths are proportional and corresponding angles are congruent. That is, dilations preserve angle measure.

A transformation that produces similar figures is a *similarity transformation*. A **similarity transformation** is a dilation or a composite of one or more dilations and one or more congruence transformations. Two figures are similar if and only if there is a similarity transformation that maps one figure to the other figure.

Determining Whether Polygons are Similar

Determine whether the polygons with the given vertices are similar.

A $A(-3, -3)$, $B(-3, 6)$, $C(6, 6)$, $D(6, -3)$
$H(-2, -2)$, $J(-2, 4)$, $K(4, 4)$, $L(4, -2)$

Yes; *ABCD* can be mapped to *HJKL*

by a dilation: $(x, y) \rightarrow \left(\frac{2}{3}x, \frac{2}{3}y\right)$.

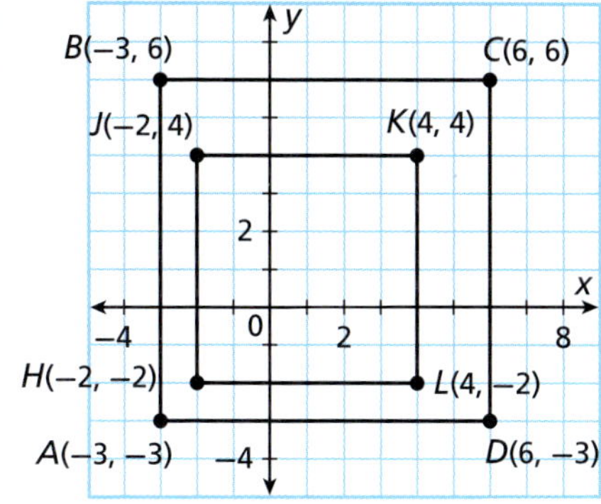

B $P(2, 2)$, $Q(2, 4)$, $R(6, 4)$, $S(6, 2)$
$W(5, 5)$, $X(5, 9)$, $Y(12, 9)$,
$Z(12, 5)$

No;

The rule $(x, y) \rightarrow (2.5x, 2.5y)$
maps *P* to *W*, but not *Q* to *X*.
No similarity transformation
maps *PQRS* to *WXYZ*.

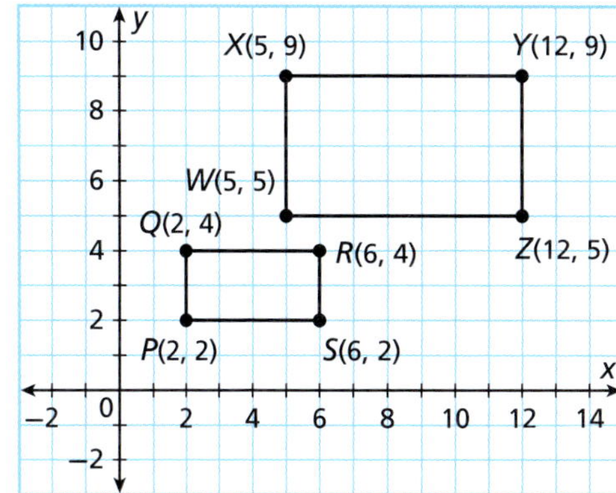

C $A(2, 1)$, $B(4, 2)$, $C(4, 1)$
$D(-9, 6)$, $E(-3, 6)$, $F(-3, 9)$

Yes; Translate $\triangle ABC$ to the left
and up. Then enlarge the
image to obtain $\triangle DEF$.

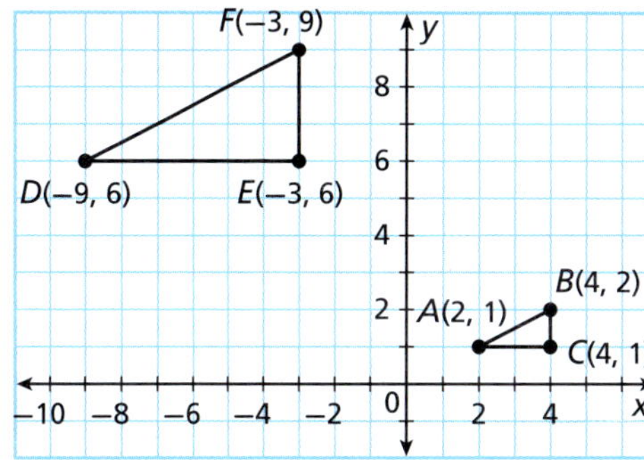

Yes; $\triangle ABC$ can be mapped to
$\triangle A'B'C'$ by a translation;
$(x, y) \rightarrow (x - 5, y + 1)$. Then
$\triangle A'B'C'$ can be mapped to
$\triangle DEF$ by a dilation:
$(x, y) \rightarrow (3x, 3y)$.

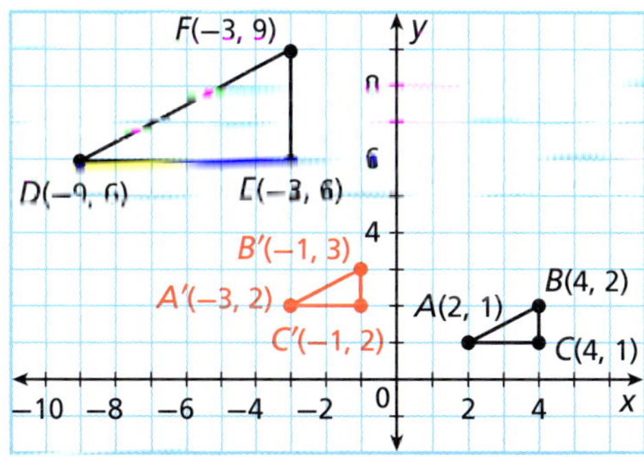

2. Determine whether the polygons with the given vertices are similar: $A(2, -1)$, $B(3, -1)$, $C(3, -4)$ and $P(3, 6)$, $Q(3, 9)$, $R(12, 9)$.

All circles are similar because they all have the same shape. To prove this, it is helpful to use a dilation whose center is not $(0, 0)$. In general, a dilation with center C and scale factor k maps P to P' so that P' is on $\overline{CP}$ and $CP' = k \cdot CP$.

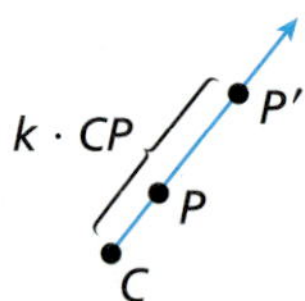

EXAMPLE 3 | **Proving Circles Similar**

A Prove that circle A with center $(0, 0)$ and radius 1 is similar to circle B with center $(5, 0)$ and radius 2.

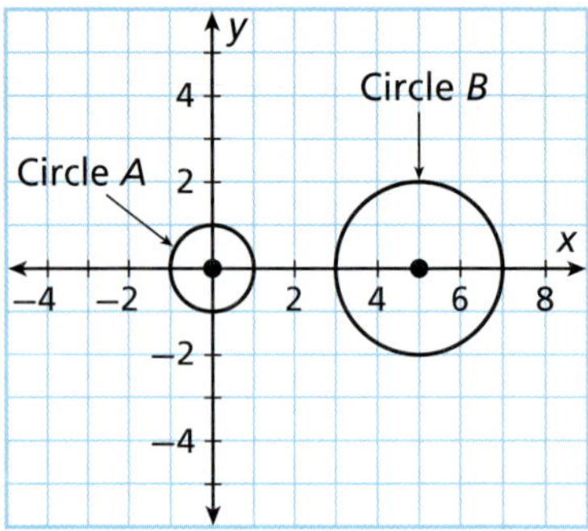

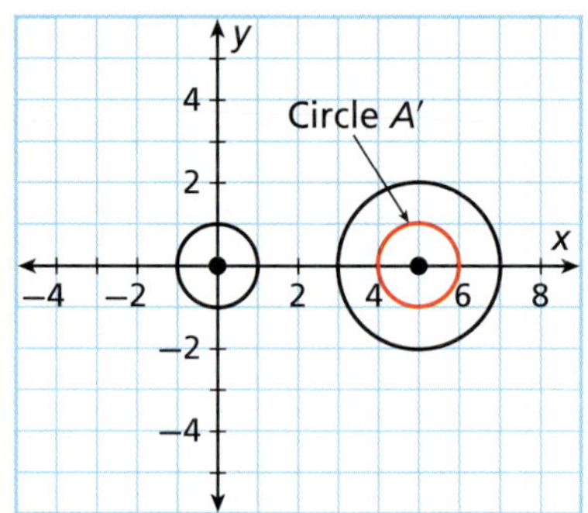

Circle A can be mapped to circle A' by a translation: $(x, y) \rightarrow (x + 5, y)$. Circle A' and circle B both have center $(5, 0)$. Then circle A' can be mapped to circle B by a dilation with center $(5, 0)$ and scale factor 2. So circles A and B are similar.

B Prove that circle C with center $(-2, 0)$ and radius 2 is similar to circle D with center $(4, 1)$ and radius 3.

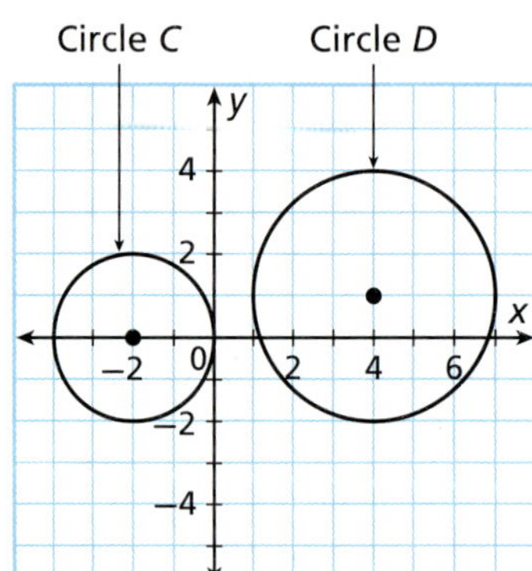

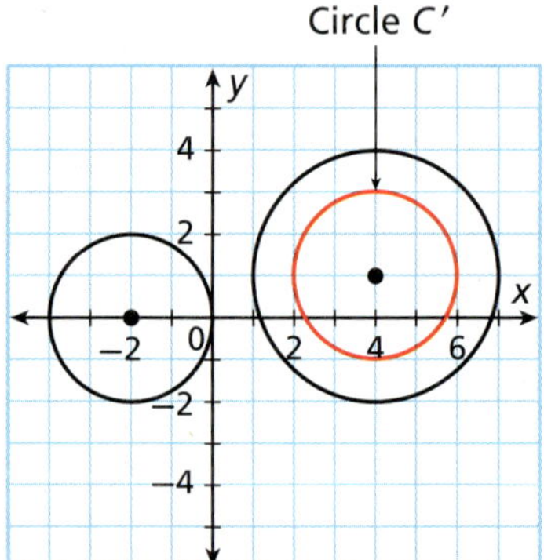

Circle C can be mapped to circle C' by a translation: $(x, y) \rightarrow (x + 6, y + 1)$. Circle C' and circle D both have center $(4, 1)$. Then circle C' can be mapped to circle D by a dilation with center $(4, 1)$ and scale factor $\frac{3}{2}$. So circles C and D are similar.

3. Prove that circle A with center $(2, 1)$ and radius 4 is similar to circle B with center $(-1, -1)$ and radius 2.

Tia makes signs and banners. She is making a banner that shows five Texas flags. The middle flag is 3 times the size of each of the other flags. Tia will first draw the lower left flag and then the middle flag. How can she draw those flags?

Place the lower left flag on a coordinate plane in a convenient position, such as that shown by rectangle *ABCD*.

Apply the dilation with center $(0, 0)$ and scale factor 3: $(x, y) \rightarrow (3x, 3y)$.

The image, $A'B'C'D'$, represents the middle flag.

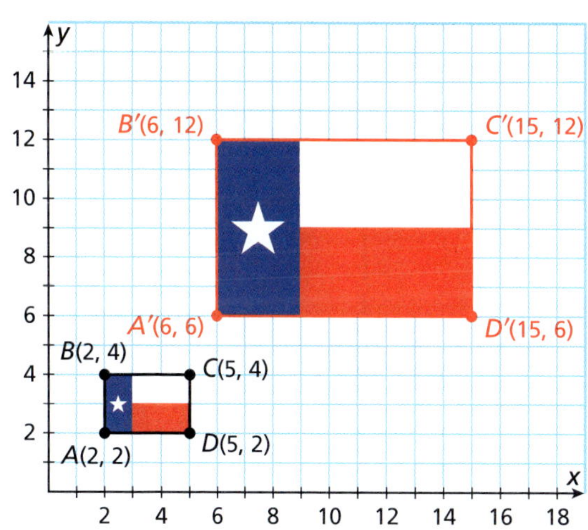

4. What if...? How could Tia draw the middle flag to make it 4 times the size of each of the other flags?

THINK AND DISCUSS

1. Consider this dilation applied to a polygon: $(x, y) \rightarrow (1.5x, 1.5y)$. Describe the corresponding side lengths, corresponding angle measures, and position of the image compared to the preimage.

2. Explain why the rules $(x, y) \rightarrow (y, -x)$ and then $(x, y) \rightarrow (2x, 2y)$ form a similarity transformation.

3. GET ORGANIZED Copy and complete the graphic organizer.

Determining if polygons are similar	
Proving circles are similar	

GUIDED PRACTICE

Vocabulary Apply the vocabulary from this lesson to answer each question.

1. A(n) ____?____ transformation produces figures that are similar. (*similarity, congruence,* or *scale factor*)

2. If the scale factor k in a dilation is a value between 0 and 1, the dilation is a(n) ____?____ . (*enlargement, reduction,* or *translation*)

SEE EXAMPLE **1**
p. CC14

Apply the dilation D to the polygon with the given vertices. Name the coordinates of the image points. Identify and describe the transformation.

3. $D : (x, y) \rightarrow (4x, 4y)$

$A(-1, -1), B(2, 1), C(-2, 1)$

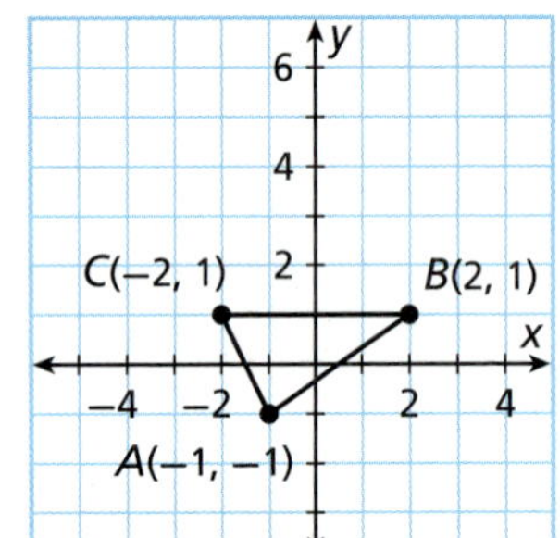

4. $D : (x, y) \rightarrow \left(\frac{1}{3}x, \frac{1}{3}y\right)$

$A(3, 9), B(-6, 3), C(3, -3)$

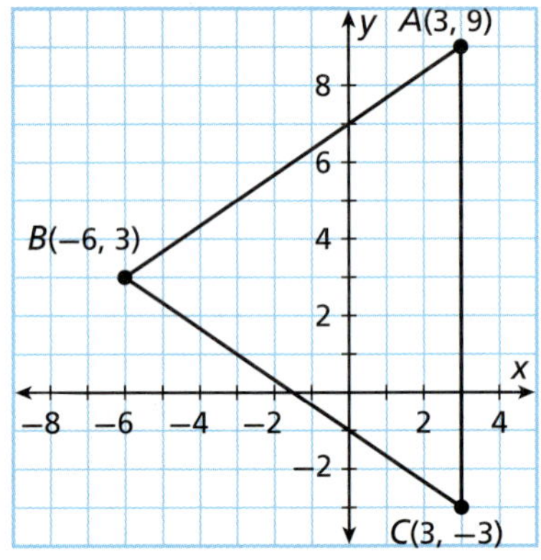

5. $D: (x, y) \rightarrow (2.5x, 2.5y)$

$A(2, 3), B(5, -2), C(-4, -2)$

6. $D: (x, y) \rightarrow \left(\frac{3}{4}x, \frac{3}{4}y\right)$

$A(4, 8), B(-8, 4), C(8, -4)$

SEE EXAMPLE **2**
p. CC15

Determine whether the polygons with the given vertices are similar. Support your answer by describing a transformation.

7. $L(1, -4), M(1, -9), N(5, -2), O(9, -5)$
$P(2, 5), Q(2, -5), R(10, 9), S(18, 3)$

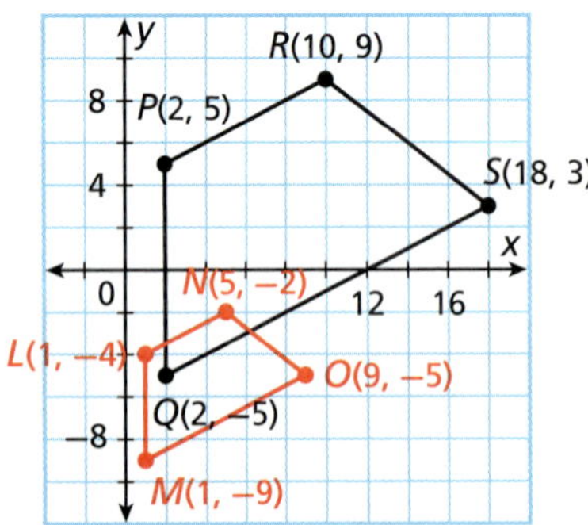

8. $W(-4, 2), X(-4, 6), Y(6, 2), Z(6, 6)$
$D(-2, 1), E(-8, 12), F(3, 10), G(3, 3)$

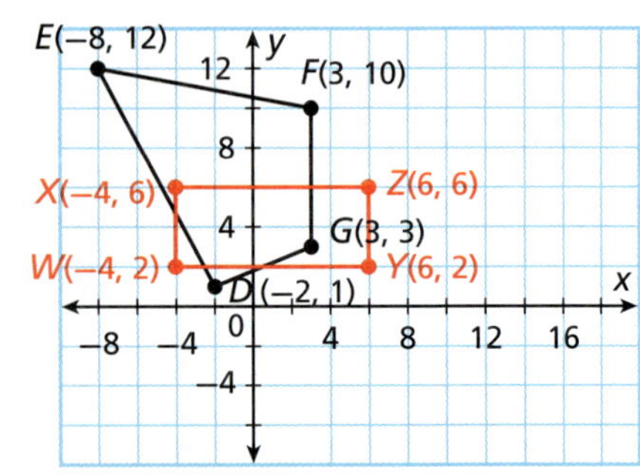

9. $A(3, 0), B(3, 6), C(9, 6)$
$X(4, 0), Y(4, -8), Z(12, -8)$

10. $L(-10, 5), M(-5, 0), N(0, 0), O(5, 5)$
$D(4, 2), E(2, 0), F(0, 0), G(-2, 2)$

11. Prove that circle A with center $(4, 0)$ and radius 5 is similar to circle B with center $(-6, -3)$ and radius 3.

12. Prove that circle A with center $(6, -9)$ and radius 4 is similar to circle B with center $(3, -8)$ and radius 5.

13. Hector is making an art project by cutting and gluing shapes to a wooden board. His design includes two similar triangles, with one 4 times the size of the other. He cuts and traces the small triangle first onto grid paper. Describe how he can use the tracing to make a pattern for the large fabric triangle.

PRACTICE AND PROBLEM SOLVING

Apply the dilation D to the polygon with the given vertices. Name the coordinates of the image points. Identify and describe the transformation.

14. $D : (x, y) \rightarrow (0.5x, 0.5y)$

$A(1, -2), B(1, -4), C(5, -2)\ D(5, -4)$

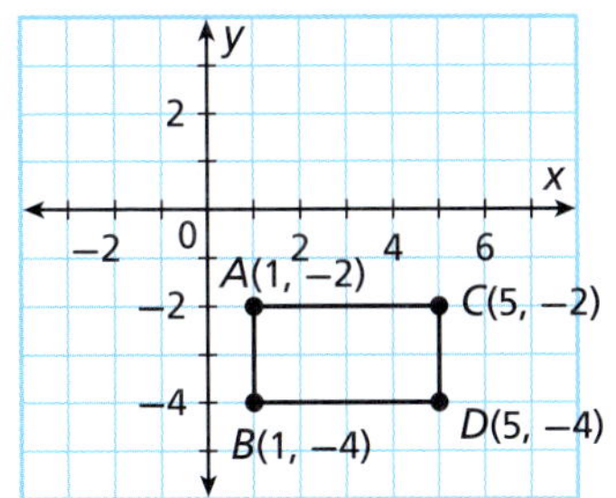

15. $D : (x, y) \rightarrow \left(\dfrac{3}{10}x, \dfrac{3}{10}y\right)$

$A(20, 10), B(0, -20), C(10, 30)$

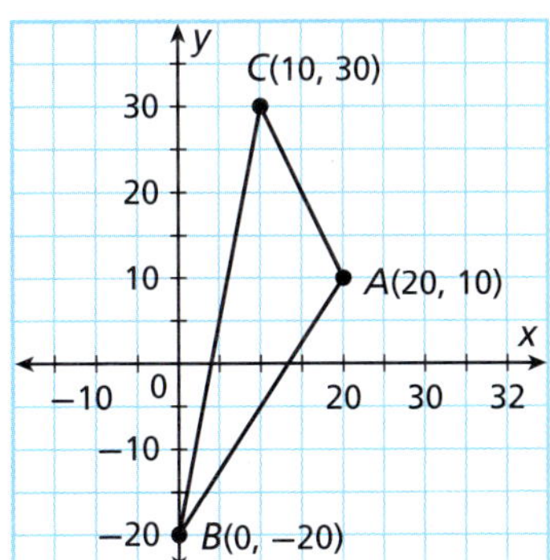

Determine whether the polygons with the given vertices are similar. Support your answer by describing a transformation.

16. $V(3, 2), W(8, 2), X(1, 5)$

$R(6, 4), S(16, 4), T(3, 15)$

17. $A(-2, -3), B(-2, 0), C(10, -3)$

$P(-4, 2), Q(-4, 4), R(4, 2)$

18. Write About It Triangle ABC is dilated by a scale factor of 5. The image is $A'B'C'$. Compare the angle measures and side lengths of the original triangle and its image after dilation.

Determine whether the polygons shown are similar. If they are similar, describe the transformation in two different ways, from the larger to the smaller figure, and from the smaller to the larger figure.

19.
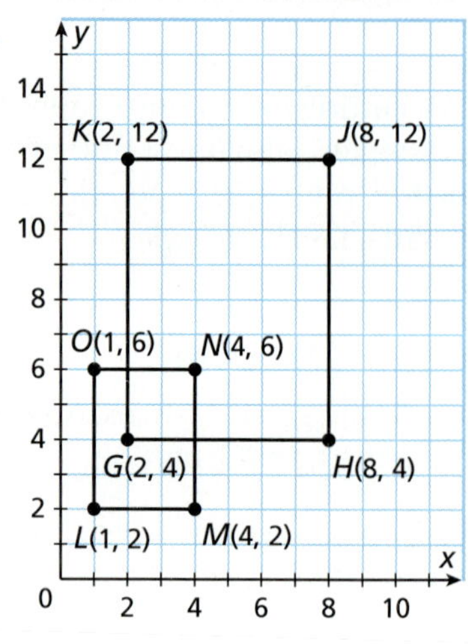

20.
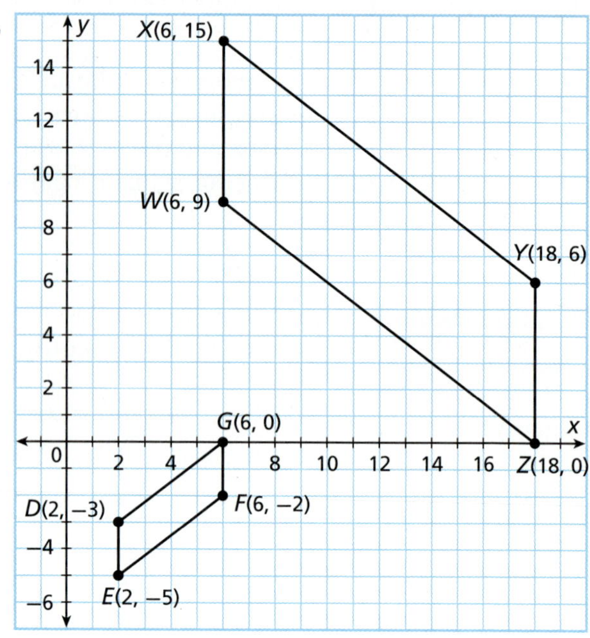

21. **///ERROR ANALYSIS///** Triangle ABC has vertices at $A(-12, -6)$, $B(-6, 12)$, and $C(6, 12)$. The images of A and B after the similarity transformation D are $A'(-8, -4)$ and $B'(-4, 8)$. Reggie and Hillary find different coordinates for C', the image of C. Their work is shown below. Who made an error? Describe the error.

Hillary's Work	Reggie's Work
$C': (6, 12) \rightarrow \left(\frac{2}{3} \cdot 6, \frac{2}{3} \cdot 12\right)$ $\rightarrow (4, 8)$	$C': (6, 12) \rightarrow \left(\frac{3}{2} \cdot 6, \frac{3}{2} \cdot 12\right)$ $\rightarrow (9, 18)$

22. A baby pool with radius 2 meters is being built near a larger pool with radius 4 meters at a recreation center. The plans for the construction are laid out on the coordinate system shown. Prove that the baby pool is similar to the larger pool.

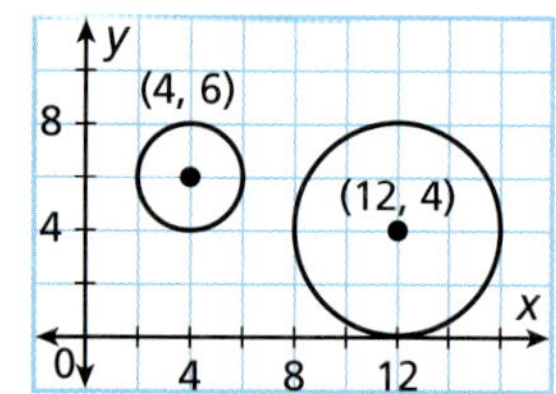

23. **Architecture** An architect is making a scale drawing of two buildings whose floor plans are to be similar rectangles. He has already drawn the smaller building. The larger building will be located to the upper right and will have dimensions 5 times those of the smaller building. How can he draw the larger building?

24. **Critical Thinking** To map a figure A to a similar figure B, first A is mapped to A' by a dilation: $(x, y) \rightarrow \left(\frac{5}{3}x, \frac{5}{3}y\right)$. Then A' is mapped to B by a translation $(x, y) \rightarrow (x - 2, y + 1)$. The vertices of A' are $W(-10, 0)$, $X(-5, 10)$, $Y(5, 10)$, and $Z(-5, 0)$. Find the vertices of A and B.

25. Triangle *ABC* undergoes a transformation *T* to produce the image *EFG*. Given the vertices of the triangles below, which is a true statement about *T*?

$$A(4, 8), B(0, 4), C(4, 0)$$
$$E(3, 6), F(0, 3), G(3, 0)$$

Ⓐ *T* is a similarity transformation in which *ABC* is dilated by a scale factor of $\frac{3}{4}$.

Ⓑ *T* is a congruence transformation in which *ABC* is dilated by a scale factor of $\frac{3}{4}$.

Ⓒ *T* is a similarity transformation in which *ABC* is dilated by a scale factor of of $\frac{4}{3}$.

Ⓓ *T* is a congruence transformation in which *ABC* is dilated by a scale factor of of $\frac{4}{3}$.

26. Figure *ABCD* with the vertices given below is translated 6 units left and 7 units down. It is then dilated to produce the similar figure *EFGH* with the vertices given below. By what scale is the figure dilated?

$$A(10, 15), B(14, 7), C(6, 7), D(6, 11)$$
$$E(5, 10), F(10, 0), G(0, 0), H(0, 5)$$

Ⓐ 0.5

Ⓑ 0.8

Ⓒ 1.25

Ⓓ 1.5

CHALLENGE AND EXTEND

27. The area of a square is 16 square units and its lower left vertex is positioned at (2, 0). After a similarity transformation, the image of the lower left vertex is positioned at (−8, 0). Name the other three vertices of the image and find its area.

28. The hypotenuse of a right triangle *ABC* in a coordinate plane is $\overline{AB}$, with *A* at (1, 2) and *B* at (3, 6). The image of the hypotenuse after a rotation of 180° and a dilation is $\overline{A'B'}$, with *A'* at (−3.5, −7) and *B'* at (−10.5, −21). Give two possible locations of *C'*, the image of *C*.

SPIRAL REVIEW

Find the distance between the two points. *(Lesson 1-6)*

29. *A*(1, 5) and *B*(9, 2)

30. *C*(−2, 3) and *D*(8, 1)

31. Write a conditional from the following sentence: You should clean your boots after you walk through mud. *(Lesson 2-2)*

32. $\overline{CD}$ is a median and *DB* = 3. What is *AB*? *(Lesson 5-3)*

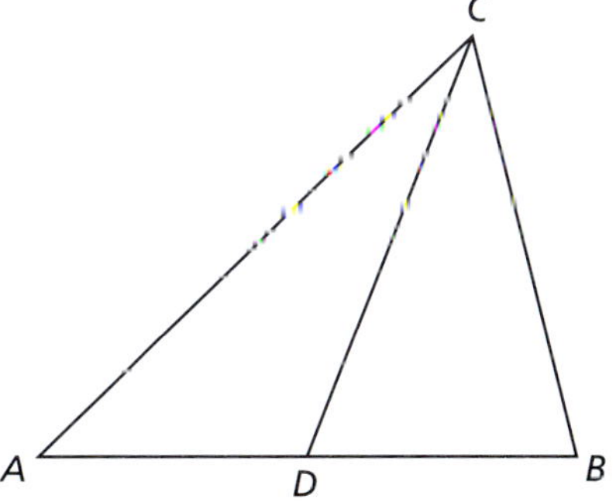

Proving the Pythagorean Theorem

Objective
Prove the Pythagorean
Theorem using similar
triangles.

The Pythagorean Theorem is one of the most widely used and well-known mathematical theorems. The theorem has been proven in many different ways, some of which involve subdividing the triangle in some way. The following proof uses similar triangles.

EXAMPLE **1**   **Proving the Pythagorean Theorem Using Similar Triangles**

Prove the Pythagorean Theorem using similar triangles.
Given: $\triangle ABC$ with right $\angle C$
Prove: $a^2 + b^2 = c^2$

Remember!

To review the altitude of a triangle, see page 316.
To review the AA similarity postulate, see page 470.

Proof: Draw an altitude from vertex C to side c as shown. By the Reflexive Property of Congruence, $\angle A \cong \angle A$ and $\angle B \cong \angle B$. All right angles are congruent, so $\angle ADC \cong \angle ACB$ and $\angle BDC \cong \angle ACB$. Therefore, $\triangle ACD \sim \triangle ABC$ and $\triangle CBD \sim \triangle ABC$ by the AA Similarity Postulate.

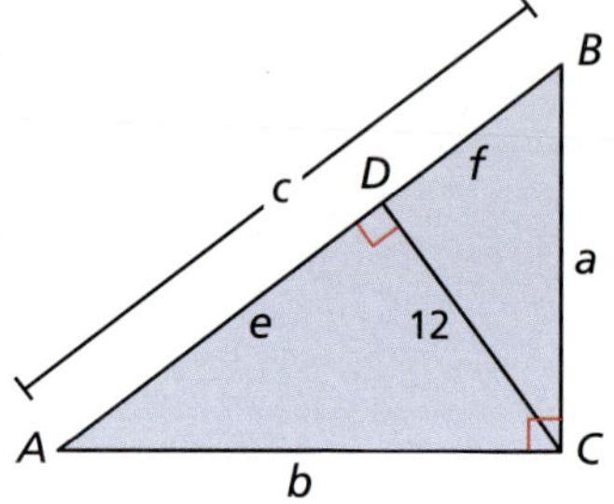

By the Transitive Property of Similarity, $\triangle ACD \sim \triangle CBD$.

Corresponding sides of similar triangles are proportional, so $\dfrac{c}{a} = \dfrac{a}{f}$ and $\dfrac{c}{b} = \dfrac{b}{e}$.

$$\dfrac{c}{a} = \dfrac{a}{f} \qquad\qquad \dfrac{c}{b} = \dfrac{b}{e}$$

$$cf = a^2 \qquad\qquad ce = b^2 \qquad \textit{Cross-multiply.}$$

$$a^2 + ce = a^2 + b^2 \qquad \textit{Add } a^2 \textit{ to both sides.}$$

$$cf + ce = a^2 + b^2 \qquad cf = a^2$$

$$c(f + e) = a^2 + b^2 \qquad \textit{Factor.}$$

$$c^2 = a^2 + b^2 \qquad c = e + f \textit{ (Segment Addition)}$$

1. In the figure, find c, e, and f.

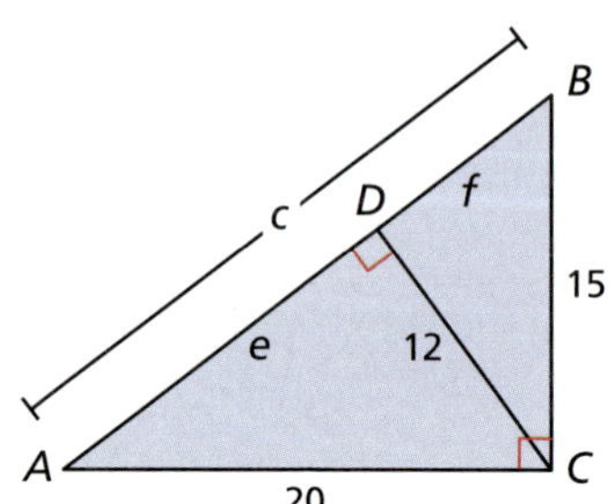

EXAMPLE 2   Applying the Pythagorean Theorem

Mike places a 20-foot ladder diagonally against the wall of the building. The bottom of the ladder is 3.5 feet from the building. The top of the ladder reaches how many feet above the ground?

Use the Pythagorean Theorem. The ladder is the hypotenuse of the triangle.

$$a^2 + b^2 = c^2$$
$$3.5^2 + b^2 = 20^2$$
$$12.25 + b^2 = 400$$
$$b^2 = 387.75$$
$$b \approx 19.7$$

The ladder reaches approximately 19.7 ft above the ground.

2. Jackie drives 5 miles east and 3 miles north from home to school. What is the shortest distance from Jackie's home to school?

EXTENSION

Exercises

Find the unknown values in each figure. Give your answers in simplest radical form.

1.

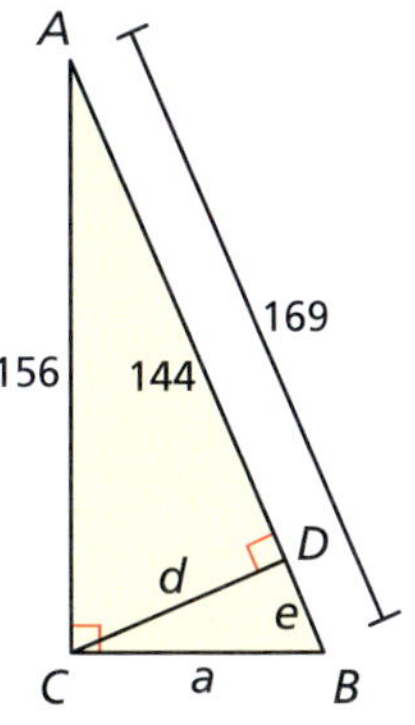

2.

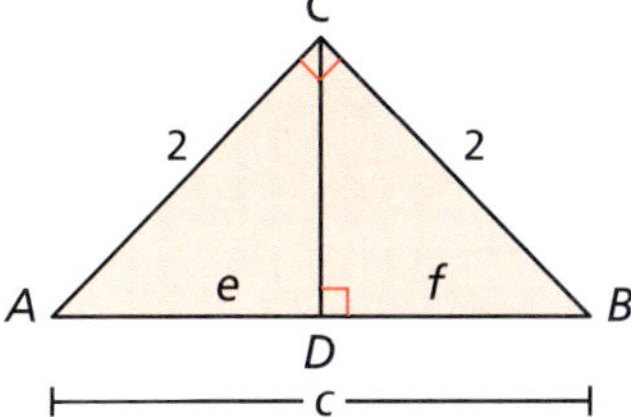

3. Critical Thinking Explain why any triple a, $2a$, $a\sqrt{3}$ are possible side lengths of a right triangle for any constant a.

4. The figure shows a loading dock with a ramp used to unload packages. What is the length of the ramp?

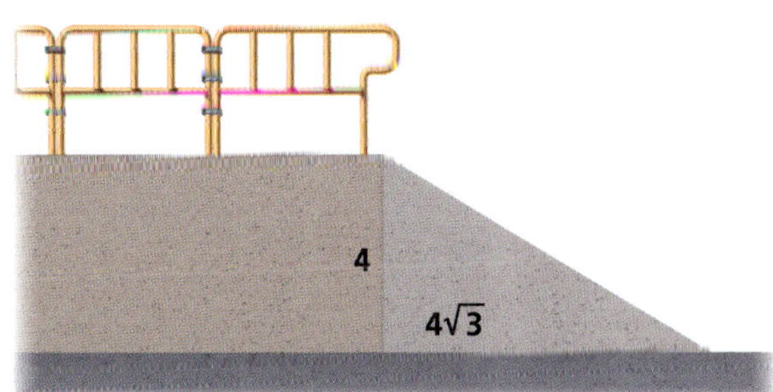

Mastering the Standards

for Mathematical Practice

The topics described in the Standards for Mathematical Content will vary from year to year. However, the *way* in which you learn, study, and think about mathematics will not. The Standards for Mathematical Practice describe skills that you will use in all of your math courses.

Mathematical Practices

1. Make sense of problems and persevere in solving them.
2. Reason abstractly and quantitatively.
3. Construct viable arguments and critique the reasoning of others.
4. Model with mathematics.
5. Use appropriate tools strategically.
6. Attend to precision.
7. Look for and make use of structure.
8. Look for and express regularity in repeated reasoning.

5 Use appropriate tools strategically.

Mathematically proficient students consider the available tools when solving a... problem... [and] are... able to use technological tools to explore and deepen their understanding...

In your book

Algebra Labs and **Technology Labs** use concrete and technological tools to explore mathematical concepts.

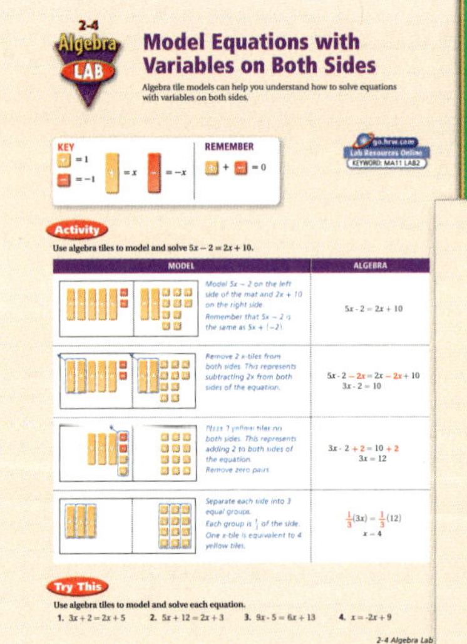
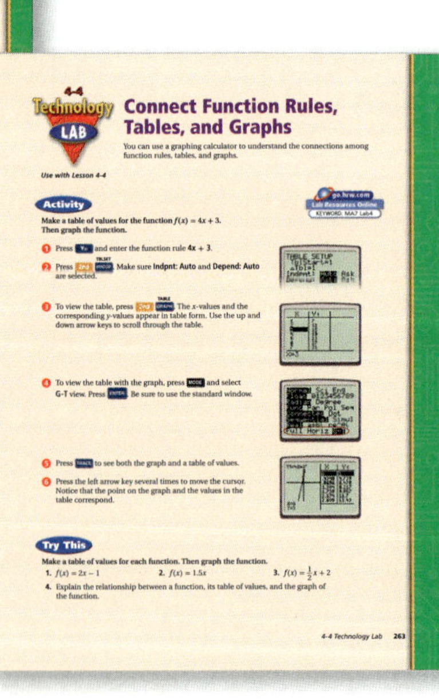

Segment Partition

Objectives
Divide a directed line segment into partitions.

A **directed line segment** is a segment between two points A and B with a specified direction, from A to B or from B to A. To partition a directed line segment is to divide it into two segments with a given ratio.

EXAMPLE 1 Finding the Coordinates of a Point in a Directed Line Segment

Vocabulary
directed line segment

Find the point P along the directed line segment from point $A(-8, -7)$ to point $B(8, 5)$ that divides the segment in the ratio 3 to 1.

First, find the rise and run of the directed line segment.

$$\text{rise} = |-7 - 5| = 12$$

$$\text{run} = |8 - (-8)| = 16$$

Point P is $\frac{3}{4}$ of the way between points A and B, so find $\frac{3}{4}$ of both the rise and the run:

$$\frac{3}{4} \text{ of rise} = \frac{3}{4}(12) = 9$$

$$\frac{3}{4} \text{ of run} = \frac{3}{4}(16) = 12$$

Remember!

In a coordinate plane, the slope of a line or segment through points (x_1, y_1) and (x_2, y_2) is $m = \dfrac{\text{rise}}{\text{run}} = \dfrac{y_2 - y_1}{x_2 - x_1}$.
(See page 182.)

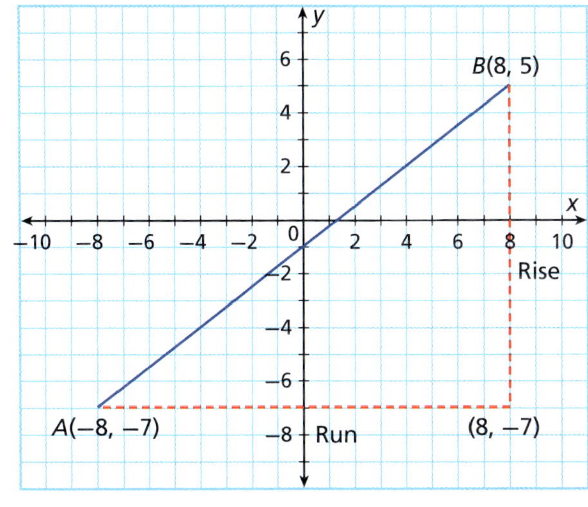

Point P is 9 units up and 12 units right from point A. Its coordinates are $(-8 + 12, -7 + 9)$, or $(4, 2)$.

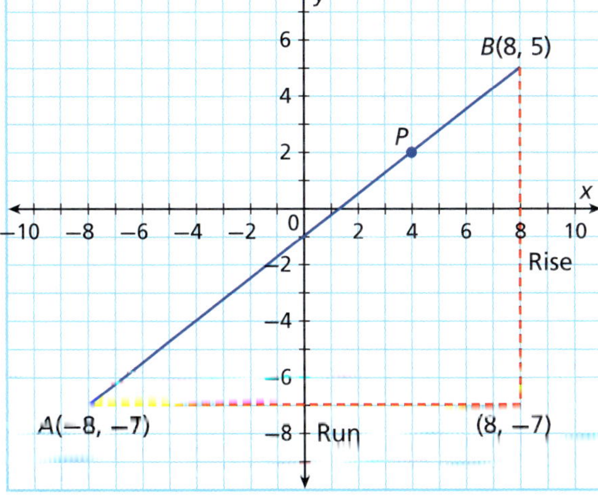

1. Find the point Q along the directed line segment from point $R(-2, 4)$ to point $S(18, -6)$ that divides the segment in the ratio 3 to 7.

Given the directed line segment from A to B, construct a point G that divides the segment in the ratio 1 to 1 from A to B.

Use a straightedge to draw the ray $\overrightarrow{AC}$. The exact measure of the angle is not important, but the construction is easiest for angles from about 30° to 60°.

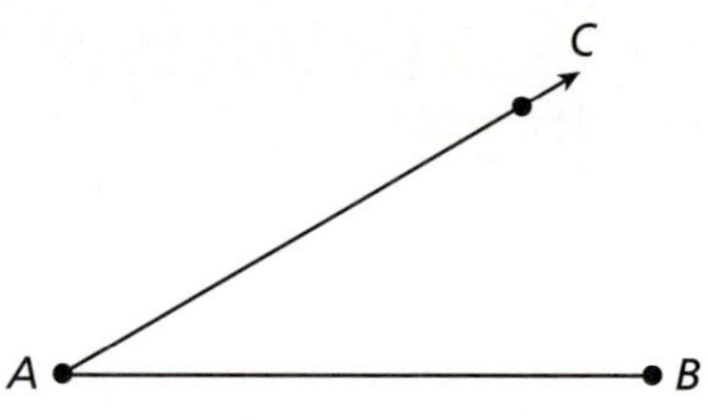

Place the compass point on A and draw an arc through $\overrightarrow{AC}$. Label the intersection D. Using the same compass setting, draw another arc centered on D, and label the intersection E.

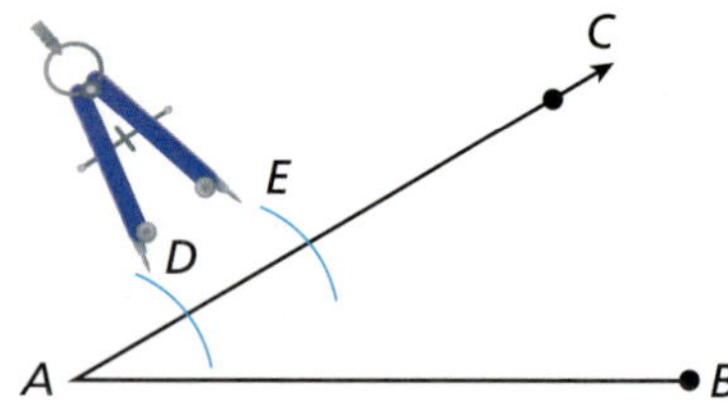

Connect points B and E. Construct an angle congruent to $\angle AEB$ with D as its vertex. Label the intersection of the angle with $\overrightarrow{AB}$ as point F.

Point F divides the segment in the ratio 1 to 1.

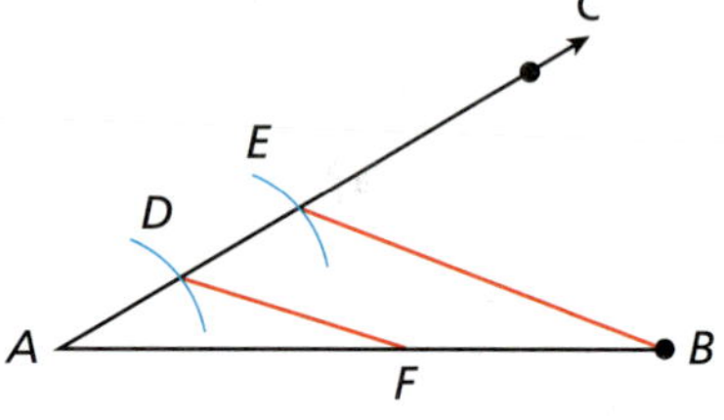

2. Draw a directed line segment from A to B, then construct point P that divides the segment in the ratio 2 to 3 from point B to point A.

EXTENSION

Exercises

1. Find the point P along the directed line segment from point A to point B that divides the segment in the ratio 2 to 5.

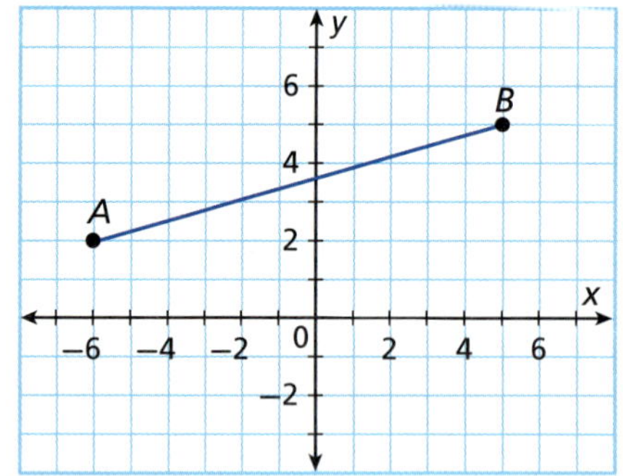

2. Find the point P along the directed line segment from point A to point B that divides the segment in the ratio 1 to 6.

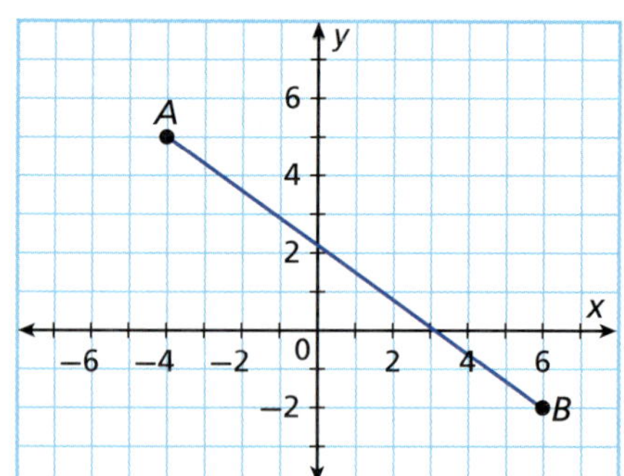

3. Draw a directed line segment from A to B, then construct point P that divides the segment in the ratio 4 to 1 from point A to point B.

Trigonometric Ratios and Complementary Angles

The acute angles of a right triangle are complementary angles (see Corollary 4-2-2). If the measure of one of the two acute angles is given, the measure of the second acute angle can be found by subtracting the given measure from 90°.

EXAMPLE 1

Finding the Sine and Cosine of Acute Angles

Vocabulary
cofunction

Find the sine and cosine of the acute angles in the right triangle shown.

Start with the sine and cosine of $\angle A$.

$$\sin A = \frac{\text{opposite}}{\text{hypotenuse}} = \frac{6}{10} = \frac{3}{5}$$

$$\cos A = \frac{\text{adjacent}}{\text{hypotenuse}} = \frac{8}{10} = \frac{4}{5}$$

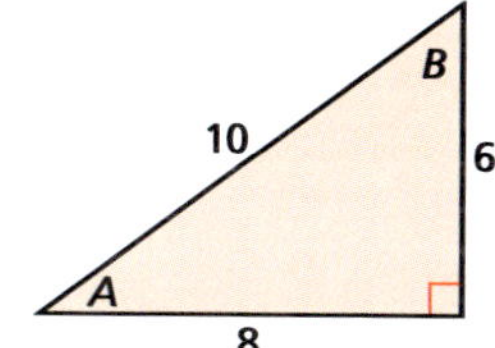

Remember!

To review complementary angles, see page 29.

To review the sine and cosine, see page 525.

Then, find the sine and cosine of $\angle B$.

$$\sin B = \frac{\text{opposite}}{\text{hypotenuse}} = \frac{8}{10} = \frac{4}{5}$$

$$\cos B = \frac{\text{adjacent}}{\text{hypotenuse}} = \frac{6}{10} = \frac{3}{5}$$

1. Find the sine and cosine of the acute angles of a right triangle with sides 10, 24, 26. (Use A for the angle opposite the side with length 10 and B for the angle opposite the side with length 24.)

In Example 1, notice that $\sin A = \cos B$ and $\cos A = \sin B$. In general, the sine of an acute angle is equal to the cosine of the complement of that angle.

The trigonometric function of the complement of an angle is called a **cofunction.** The sine and cosines are cofunctions of each other.

EXAMPLE 2

Writing Sine in Cosine Terms and Cosine in Sine Terms

A Write sin 42° in terms of the cosine.

$$\sin 42° = \cos(90 - 42)°$$
$$= \cos 48°$$

B Write cos 36° in terms of the sine.

$$\cos 36° = \sin(90 - 36)°$$
$$= \sin 54°$$

2a. Write sin 28° in terms of the cosine.

2b. Write cos 51° in terms of the sine.

Find two angles that satisfy the equation.

$$\sin(2x - 4)° = \cos(3x + 9)°$$

If $\sin(2x - 4)° = \cos(3x + 9)°$, then $(2x - 4)°$ and $(3x + 9)°$ are the measures of complementary angles. The sum of the measures must be 90°.

$$(2x - 4) + (3x + 9) = 90$$
$$5x + 5 = 90$$
$$5x = 85$$
$$x = 17$$

Substitute the value of x into the original expression to find the angle measures.

$$2x - 4 = 2(17) - 4$$
$$= 30°$$

$$3x + 9 = 3(17) + 9$$
$$= 60°$$

The measurements of the two angles are 30° and 60°.

Find the two angles that satisfy the equation

3a. $\sin(3x + 2)° = \cos(x + 44)°$.

3b. $\sin(2x + 20)° = \cos(3x + 30)°$.

EXTENSION

Exercises

Find the cosine and sine of the acute angles in the triangles shown.

1. 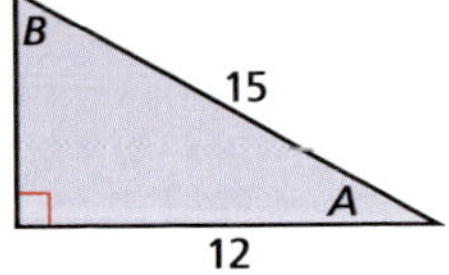

2. 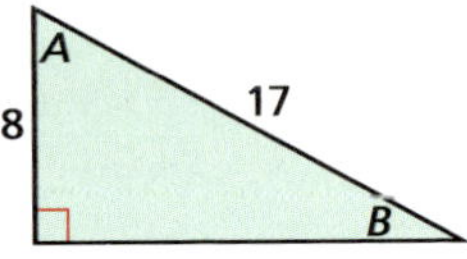

Write each trigonometric function in terms of its cofunction.

3. sin 64°

4. cos 84°

5. cos 38°

6. sin 24°

7. cos 72°

8. sin 45°

Find two angles that satisfy each equation.

9. $\sin(4x + 30)° = \cos(-2x + 54)°$

10. $\sin(-2x + 92)° = \cos(x + 8)°$

11. $\cos(5x + 49)° = \sin(3x + 57)°$

12. $\cos(-3x + 106)° = \sin(7x - 64)°$

13. $\sin(2x + 30)° = \cos(3x + 5)°$

14. $\sin(5x - 12)° = \cos(x + 54)°$

15. $\cos(3x - 10)° = \sin(3x - 20)°$

16. $\cos(7x - 68)° = \sin(-3x + 110)°$

Mastering the Standards

for Mathematical Practice

The topics described in the Standards for Mathematical Content will vary from year to year. However, the *way* in which you learn, study, and think about mathematics will not. The Standards for Mathematical Practice describe skills that you will use in all of your math courses.

Mathematical Practices

1. *Make sense of problems and persevere in solving them.*
2. *Reason abstractly and quantitatively.*
3. *Construct viable arguments and critique the reasoning of others.*
4. *Model with mathematics.*
5. *Use appropriate tools strategically.*
6. *Attend to precision.*
7. *Look for and make use of structure.*
8. *Look for and express regularity in repeated reasoning.*

4 Model with mathematics.

Mathematically proficient students can apply... mathematics... to... problems... in everyday life, society, and the workplace...

In your book

Multi-Step Test Prep and **Real-World Connections** apply mathematics to other disciplines and in real-world scenarios.

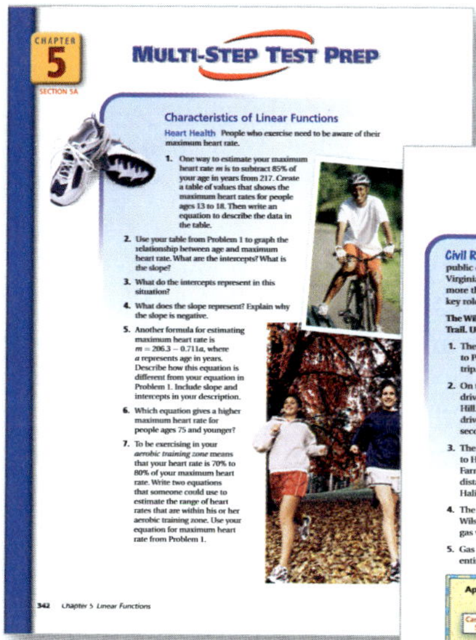

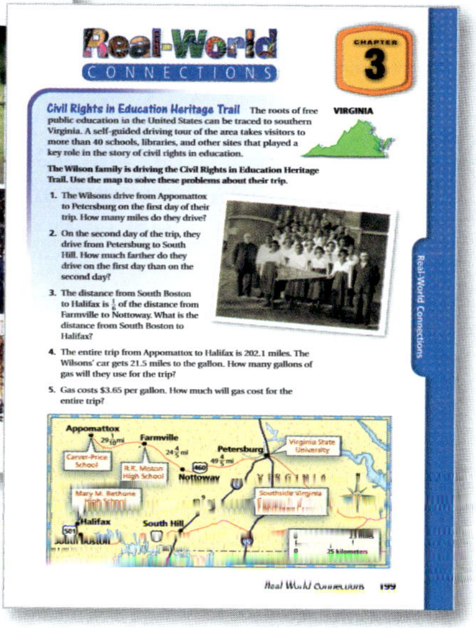

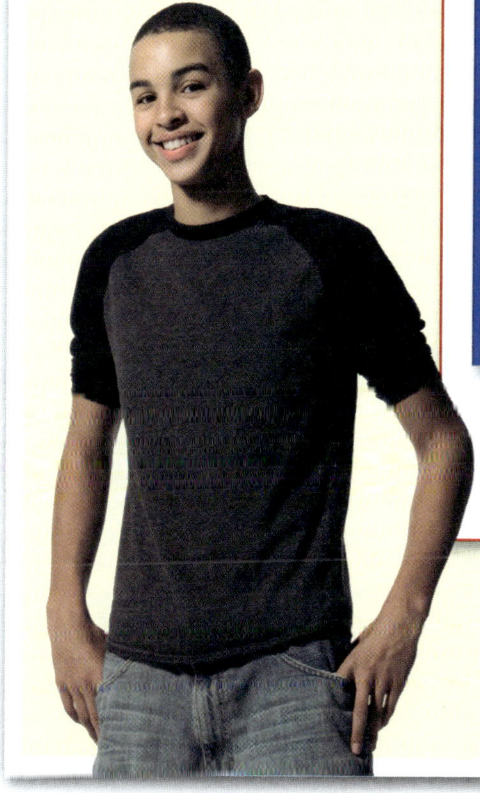

Measuring Angles in Radians

Objective
Use proportions to convert angle measures from degrees to radians.

Vocabulary
radian

One unit of measurement for angles is degrees, which are based on a fraction of a circle. Another unit is called a *radian*, which is based on the relationship of the radius and arc length of a central angle in a circle.

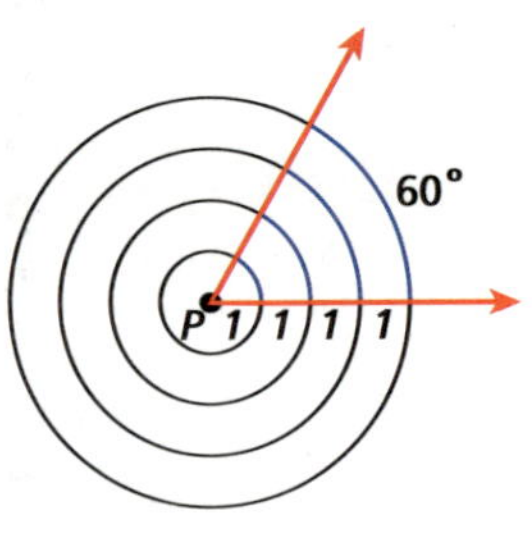

Four concentric circles are shown, with radius 1, 2, 3, and 4. The measure of each arc is 60°.

Radius	Arc Length
1	$2\pi(1)\left(\dfrac{60°}{360°}\right) = \dfrac{\pi}{3}$
2	$2\pi(2)\left(\dfrac{60°}{360°}\right) = \dfrac{2\pi}{3}$
3	$2\pi(3)\left(\dfrac{60°}{360°}\right) = \pi$
4	$2\pi(4)\left(\dfrac{60°}{360°}\right) = \dfrac{4\pi}{3}$

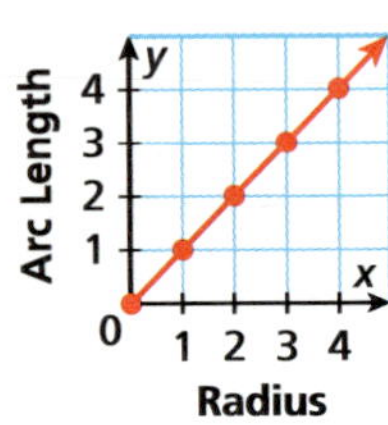

Remember!

Arc length is the distance along an arc measured in linear units. In a circle of radius r, the length of an arc with a central angle measure m is
$$L = 2\pi r\left(\frac{m°}{360°}\right).$$

See page 766.

The relationship between the radius and arc length is linear, with a slope of $2\pi\left(\frac{60°}{360°}\right) = \frac{\pi}{3}$, or about 1.05. The slope represents the ratio of the arc length to the radius. This ratio is the *radian* measure of the angle, so 60° is the same as $\frac{\pi}{3}$ radians.

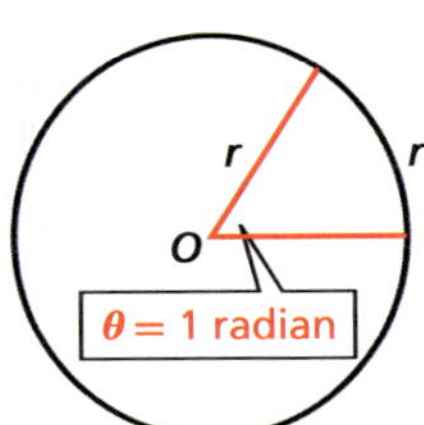

If a central angle θ in a circle of radius r intercepts an arc of length r, the measure of θ is defined as 1 **radian.** Since the circumference of a circle of radius r is $2\pi r$, an angle representing one complete rotation measures 2π radians, or 360°.

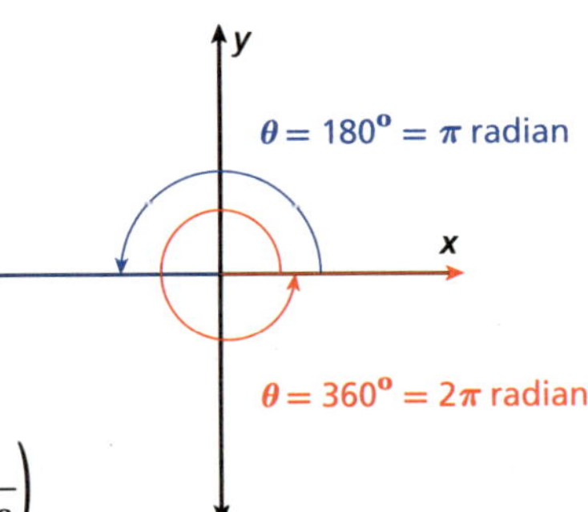

$$2\pi \text{ radians} = 360° \quad \text{and} \quad \pi \text{ radians} = 180°$$

$$1° = \left(\frac{\pi \text{ radians}}{180°}\right) \quad \text{and} \quad 1 \text{ radian} = \left(\frac{180°}{\pi \text{ radians}}\right)$$

Use these facts to convert between radians and degrees.

Converting Angle Measures	
DEGREES TO RADIANS	**RADIANS TO DEGREES**
Multiply the number of degrees by	Multiply the number of radians by
$\left(\dfrac{\pi \text{ radians}}{180°}\right)$	$\left(\dfrac{180°}{\pi \text{ radians}}\right)$

EXAMPLE 1 — Converting Degrees to Radians

Convert each measure from degrees to radians. *Multiply by $\left(\dfrac{\pi \text{ radians}}{180°}\right)$.*

Helpful Hint

Because the radian measure of an angle is related to arc length, the most commonly used angle measures are usually written as fractional multiples of π.

A 30°

$$\overset{1}{\cancel{30°}}\left(\dfrac{\pi \text{ radians}}{\underset{6}{\cancel{180°}}}\right) = \dfrac{\pi}{6} \text{ radians}$$

B 75°

$$\overset{5}{\cancel{75°}}\left(\dfrac{\pi \text{ radians}}{\underset{12}{\cancel{180°}}}\right) = \dfrac{5\pi}{12} \text{ radians}$$

CHECK IT OUT! Convert each measure from degrees to radians.

1a. −36° **1b.** 270°

EXAMPLE 2 — Converting Radians to Degrees

Convert each measure from radians to degrees.

A $\dfrac{\pi}{4}$ radians

$$\dfrac{\pi}{\underset{1}{\cancel{4}}}\text{ radians}\left(\dfrac{\overset{45}{\cancel{180°}}}{\pi \text{ radians}}\right) = 45°$$

B $\dfrac{2\pi}{9}$ radians *Multiply by $\left(\dfrac{180°}{\pi \text{ radians}}\right)$.*

$$\dfrac{2\pi}{\underset{1}{\cancel{9}}}\text{ radians}\left(\dfrac{\overset{20}{\cancel{180°}}}{\pi \text{ radians}}\right) = 40°$$

CHECK IT OUT! Convert each measure from radians to degrees.

2a. $\dfrac{5\pi}{6}$ radians **2b.** $-\dfrac{3\pi}{4}$ radians

EXTENSION Exercises

1. Convert each measure from degrees to radians to complete the table.

0°	30°	45°	60°	90°	180°	270°	360°

Convert each measure from degrees to radians.

2. 215° **3.** 25° **4.** −180° **5.** 35°

6. 120° **7.** −315° **8.** 400° **9.** −60°

Convert each measure from radians to degrees.

10. $\dfrac{6\pi}{5}$ radians **11.** $\dfrac{3\pi}{5}$ radians **12.** $-\dfrac{\pi}{3}$ radians **13.** $\dfrac{5\pi}{9}$ radians

14. $\dfrac{\pi}{6}$ radians **15.** $\dfrac{2\pi}{3}$ radians **16.** $\dfrac{3\pi}{8}$ radians **17.** $\dfrac{7\pi}{2}$ radians

18. Electronics A DVD rotates through an angle of 20π radians in 1 second. At this speed, how many revolutions does the DVD make in 2 minutes?

19. Clocks Find the measure of the angle in radians formed by the minute hand on a clock at 7:35 and its position 15 minutes later.

20. Wheels A bicycle's wheel spins backwards, making 2 complete counterclockwise revolutions. What is the measure of the wheel's rotation angle in radians?